CHARLESTON

SOUTH CARO

Come, let this special destination enliven your senses.

Explore Charleston

Livable statements start here.

WESLEY HALL
classic made current

BENCHMADE UPHOLSTERY   HICKORY/HIGH POINT   WESLEYHALL.COM

revolution
PERFORMANCE FABRICS

From the Editor

t's our birthday—the big 3-0! Of course, we're celebrating. We're celebrating our years and our mission of bringing you classic, timeless, traditional design. We're also having a little fun with the fact that we're marking this milestone along with a large slice of the millennial generation. Yep, we're millennial—old enough to recognize refined style, authenticity, and quality when we see it but nowhere near being feted with a dark cloud of "over the hill" birthday balloons.

To toast our past, our present, and our future, we bring you an issue that includes designers we've loved for years and new talents—including 10 rising stars of design. Our 2019 class of New Trads (page 32) speaks fluent classicism—in today's fresh vernacular.

Two of our New Trads, Lindsey Coral Harper and Mallory Mathison Glenn, were among an enviable list of designers who created rooms for our 2018 Southern Style Now Designer Showhouse in Charleston (page 70). When you see how they respected the history of an 1840s Greek Revival home while revitalizing it for modern living, you'll know that the future of traditional design is in good hands.

We're heartened when these new talents tell us they find endless inspiration in the work of design legends. So do we.

Think you know what to expect from kitchen design luminary Mick De Giulio? Think again. First he refines the kitchen, then he builds an entire genre-melding, boundary-melting home around it in "Kitchen 2.0" (page 88).

Likewise, designer Ray Booth of the legendary McAlpine design firm somehow magically combines British grace and American gregariousness in an early 1900s Colonial Revival home ("Light at Heart," page 96). This veritable Audrey Hepburn of Baltimore estates keeps its history as it learns to live for today.

Then there's 2017 New Trad Amy Meier, who helps past and present, classic and clean-lined intersect beautifully in a new California home ("Best of Both," page 108). Built on the site of La Jolla's original train station, it thoughtfully displays details you'd find in a New England Colonial as it wriggles its toes in the sand with the casual ease of a beach bungalow.

As these designers and these homes prove, celebrating our past is good—especially when we also celebrate our future.

Jill

Jill Waage, Editor in Chief
traditionalhome@meredith.com

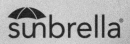

DESIGN + PERFORMANCE™

Design + Performance™ is a trademark, Legendary Performance Fabrics; and Sunbrella are registered trademarks of Glen Raven, Inc.

LEGENDARY PERFORMANCE FABRICS

SUNBRELLA.COM   FADE PROOF / EASY CARE / BLEACH CLEANABLE

KINGS✦HAVEN

TRADITIONAL HOME.

JILL WAAGE
EDITOR IN CHIEF

EXECUTIVE EDITOR **MARSHA A. RAISCH**
ART DIRECTOR **MICK SCHNEPF**

EDITORIAL
SENIOR DESIGN & LIFESTYLE EDITOR **JENNY BRADLEY PFEFFER**
SENIOR STYLE EDITOR **KRISSA ROSSBUND**
SENIOR ARCHITECTURE & DESIGN EDITOR **SALLY FINDER WEEPIE**
ASSOCIATE STYLE & SOCIAL MEDIA EDITOR **CLARA HANEBERG**
MARKETS & SOCIAL MEDIA EDITOR **ANNA LOGAN**
CONTRIBUTING FOOD EDITOR **SHELLI McCONNELL**
EDITORIAL ASSISTANT **KIM O'BRIEN-WOLETT**
EDITORIAL APPRENTICE **TARA LARSON**
CONTRIBUTING COPY EDITORS **KATHLEEN ARMENTROUT, NANCY DIETZ**

ART
PHOTOGRAPHY COORDINATOR **ALYSSA RICHARDSON**

PREPRESS DESKTOP SPECIALISTS **GREG FAIRHOLM, BRIAN FRANK, STEVE LAUSE**
PHOTO STUDIO MANAGER **DAVE DeCARLO**
TEST KITCHEN DIRECTOR **LYNN BLANCHARD**

CONTRIBUTORS
EDITOR AT LARGE **ELEANOR ROPER**
INTERIOR DESIGN **CATHY WHITLOCK**
FOOD/ENTERTAINING **CHEF MARY PAYNE MORAN**

ATLANTA **LISA MOWRY**
BALTIMORE **EILEEN A. DEYMIER**
BOSTON **ESTELLE BOND GURALNICK**
CHARLESTON, SC **SANDRA L. MOHLMANN**
CHARLOTTE, NC **ANDREA CAUGHEY**
CHICAGO **ELAINE MARKOUTSAS, HILARY ROSE**
CONNECTICUT **STACY KUNSTEL**
FLORIDA **ELEANOR LYNN NESMITH**
LOS ANGELES **DARRA BAKER**
NEW ORLEANS **MARGARET ZAINEY ROUX**
NEW YORK **BONNIE MAHARAM**
PARIS **LYNN McBRIDE**
PORTLAND, OR **BARBARA MUNDALL**
SAN FRANCISCO **HEATHER LOBDELL**
SEATTLE **LINDA HUMPHREY**

EDITORIAL OFFICES
DES MOINES | 1716 LOCUST STREET, DES MOINES, IA 50309-3023
NEW YORK | 225 LIBERTY STREET, 9TH FLOOR, NEW YORK, NY 10281
E-MAIL TRADITIONALHOME@MEREDITH.COM
We assume no responsibility for unsolicited manuscripts or art materials.

BETH McDONOUGH
PUBLISHER

STACEY FARRAR-HERMES EXECUTIVE BRAND DIRECTOR, INTEGRATED MARKETING

ADVERTISING
VICTORIA HUBBARD CARRA SENIOR ACCOUNT MANAGER
TYLER J. HUB SALES DIRECTOR, DIRECT MEDIA
BREANA TOLLA ASSOCIATE BUSINESS DEVELOPMENT MANAGER
MELISSA LUEBBE NATIONAL TRAVEL DIRECTOR
JESSICA LEVINE BUSINESS MANAGER
SOPHIA THID ASSOCIATE SALES AND MARKETING MANAGER
CHERYL CORBIN ADVERTISING SALES ASSISTANT

SUZANNE COOPER–SCOOP MEDIA ATLANTA, SOUTHEAST
TRACY SZAFARZ CHICAGO, MIDWEST, TEXAS, AND CANADA
MARK ROSENBAUM CHICAGO, MIDWEST
KAREN BARNHART, WENDY ROSINSKI, DIANE PAGLINO DETROIT
MOLLY WOOTTON LOS ANGELES, WEST COAST
BLAIR SHALES LOS ANGELES SALES AND MARKETING COORDINATOR

NEW YORK 212/522-5555 | ATLANTA 770/998-0996 | CHICAGO 312/580-1619
DALLAS 312/580-1618 | DETROIT 248/205-2570 | LOS ANGELES 310/689-1695
TRAVEL 212/499-6704 | DIRECT MEDIA 212/499-6778

INTEGRATED MARKETING
CHRISTINE STALEY CORR PROMOTION DIRECTOR, INTEGRATED MARKETING
KIM LeCONEY DIRECTOR, SALES STRATEGY & INSIGHTS
CHERYL CAMPBELL SENIOR RESEARCH MANAGER

STEPHEN BOHLINGER SENIOR VICE PRESIDENT/GROUP PUBLISHER

GRAHAM WOODWARD CONSUMER MARKETING MANAGER
KENT POLLPETER PRODUCTION DIRECTOR
COURTNEY BEBENSEE PRODUCTION MANAGER
JULIE MOORE SENIOR BUSINESS MANAGER

MEREDITH NATIONAL MEDIA GROUP
DOUG OLSON PRESIDENT, MEREDITH MAGAZINES
TOM WITSCHI PRESIDENT, CONSUMER PRODUCTS
CATHERINE LEVENE PRESIDENT, CHIEF DIGITAL OFFICER
MICHAEL BROWNSTEIN CHIEF REVENUE OFFICER
ALYSIA BORSA CHIEF MARKETING & DATA OFFICER
NANCY WEBER MARKETING & INTEGRATED COMMUNICATIONS

SENIOR VICE PRESIDENTS
ANDY WILSON CONSUMER REVENUE
BRIAN KIGHTLINGER CORPORATE SALES
PATTI FOLLO DIRECT MEDIA
BRITTA CLEVELAND RESEARCH SOLUTIONS
CHUCK HOWELL STRATEGIC SOURCING, NEWSSTAND, PRODUCTION
MARLA NEWMAN DIGITAL SALES
MATT PETERSEN THE FOUNDRY
JUSTIN LAW PRODUCT & TECHNOLOGY

VICE PRESIDENTS
CHRIS SUSIL FINANCE
ROB SILVERSTONE BUSINESS PLANNING & ANALYSIS
STEVE CROWE CONSUMER MARKETING
CAROL CAMPBELL SHOPPER MARKETING
STEVE GRUNE BRAND LICENSING

STEPHEN ORR VICE PRESIDENT, GROUP EDITORIAL DIRECTOR
GREG KAYKO DIRECTOR, EDITORIAL OPERATIONS & FINANCE

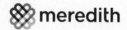

MEREDITH CORPORATION
PRESIDENT & CHIEF EXECUTIVE OFFICER **TOM HARTY**
CHIEF FINANCIAL OFFICER **JOSEPH CERYANEC**
CHIEF DEVELOPMENT OFFICER **JOHN ZIESER**
PRESIDENT, MEREDITH LOCAL MEDIA GROUP **PATRICK MCCREERY**
SENIOR VICE PRESIDENT, HUMAN RESOURCES **DINA NATHANSON**

CHAIRMAN **STEPHEN M. LACY**
VICE CHAIRMAN **MELL MEREDITH FRAZIER**

We Make ELECTRIC ...Too.

BEVOLO
– established 1945 –
GAS & ELECTRIC LIGHTS

Contents

SEPTEMBER | OCTOBER 2019

VOLUME XXX ISSUE V

96

CELEBRATING 50 YEARS OF HANDCRAFTED AMERICAN MADE FURNITURE
FROM SEAT TO SHINING SEAT

LEEINDUSTRIES.COM

40

57

Contents

September | October 2019

62

24

20

On the cover:
Charleston showhouse room designed
by Mallory Mathison Glenn;
photographed by
Katie Charlotte Fiedler. See page 70.

traditionalhome.com

It's time to *fall* back into the groove of indoor living. Get inspired by the season and refresh your rooms.

Fall in Love with Autumn Hues

Step 1: Grab a throw blanket. Step 2: Pour a mug of tea. Step 3: Settle in to enjoy all the cozy vibes in our best warm-colored rooms of all time. *TraditionalHome.com/FallColors*

Walk-In Closets That Wow

Combat closet clutter. Check out seven epic walk-in closets that will motivate you to get your shoes, shirts, and stray pieces organized. *TraditionalHome.com/Closets*

Tour These Baths, Feel Like You're at a Fancy Spa

Get your daily dose of zen at *TraditionalHome .com/SpaBaths*, where we're showcasing the calmest, most luxurious bathrooms we've ever featured. We promise these rooms will wash away all the cares of the day—and maybe inspire an awesome bathroom makeover.

RISING STARS OF DESIGN
new TRADS
• EST 2009 •
RISING STARS OF DESIGN

Meet the New Trads

Our New Trads class of 2019 has been announced! Sit down for Q&As with these 10 rising stars of design. *Traditional Home.com/ MeetTheTrads*

FOLLOW US: Facebook **facebook.com/tradhome** Twitter **@traditionalhome** Instagram **@traditionalhome** Pinterest **pinterest.com/traditionalhome**

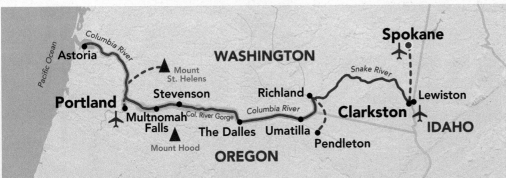

life AGLOW®

HINKLEY
LIGHTING

movers & makers

FRESH DESIGNS AND THE MINDS BEHIND THEM

WEARING IT WELL

Talk about a style icon. Tillett Textiles' "Daisy" fabric dressed Jackie Kennedy's White House bedroom. In a fresh colorway, it still turns heads—and so does the small but mighty screen-printing house in the Berkshires, now with a fourth generation at the helm. "It's a calling," Patrick McBride says. "I consider myself a steward of something bigger than me." (*t4fabrics.com*)

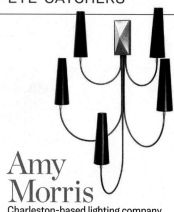

Amy Morris

Charleston-based lighting company Avrett tapped 2011 New Trad Amy Morris for its latest designer collaboration. Her eight-piece Facet collection includes lanterns, chandeliers, and sconces that take cues from fashion and French Modern antiques. The "Vogue" sconce was inspired by a Paris flea market find. "This piece can be the art in a room," Morris says. "Nothing else is needed." (*avrett.com*)

Alexa Hampton
FOR THEODORE ALEXANDER

Influenced by her travels—specifically the architectural shapes discovered in Morocco, India, and the Middle East—Alexa Hampton designed a timeless, multifaceted collection for Theodore Alexander. "I am perpetually inspired by the classics, which, of course, make many cameos in this collection," Hampton says. Usable yet unique, the 120-piece assortment includes the upholstered "Maria" dining chair with gilt detailing and the sculptural "Ingrid" side table. (*theodorealexander.com*)

Mitchell Black

Founded by Chicagoan Lynai Jones, American-made home decor brand Mitchell Black is a resource for custom and bespoke wallpaper and more. The geometric "Formation" wallcovering in Yves Blue is part of the Mrs. Paranjape Papers collection. "It masters timeless design in a refreshing way," Jones says. (*mitchellblack.com*)

Teil Duncan

With more than 85,000 followers on Instagram, Teil Duncan, known for her abstract paintings in surprising color combos, is making an impression. Duncan depicts architecture, animals, and the human form with her signature pixilated play on light. "If it's in nice light, I want to paint it," she says. "Even if it's an old shoe!" Her Figure Studies collection is a grouping of small canvases that showcase her color palette. (*teilduncan.com*)

Joanna Manousis

British-born artist Joanna Manousis has elevated glass to fine art. Her signature methods are evident in her "Parr Diamonds" installation. Inspired by St. Mary's Church at Sudeley Castle, the wall display employs cast crystal, glass, stainless steel, and oil paint to achieve a delicate design that tricks the eye. (*toddmerrillstudio.com*)

Lori Weitzner FOR ARTISTIC TILE

Drawing on her command of textile design techniques, such as pleating, origami, and voided velvet, Lori Weitzner has teamed with Artistic Tile to create a new line of surfacing. "River," *above*, and a complementary design, "Forest," convey a fabric-like effect using etched detail on natural stone. "My design style is very tactile," Weitzner says. "I don't just want people to look at a product. I want people to experience it." (*artistictile.com*)

BOBBY McALPINE
FOR LEE INDUSTRIES

Known for his sumptuous and supremely handsome interiors, architect Bobby McAlpine has set the bar high with his new McAlpine Home collection for Lee Industries. "My intent was to create a cast of characters or best supporting actors, allowing designers to use them over and over again," McAlpine says. The "1981-01" dining chair with vented barrel back, he says, "is the kind of chair you'd want your portrait done in." (*leeindustries.com*)

WRITTEN BY CLARA HANEBERG

THEODORE ALEXANDER

The Alexa Hampton Collection

theodorealexander.com

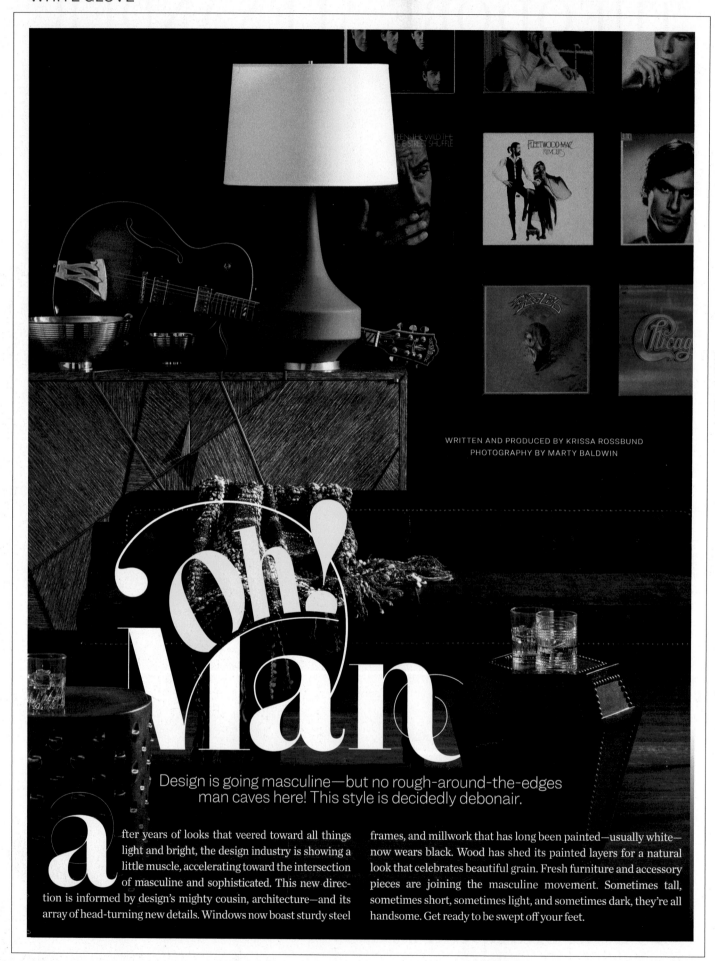

WRITTEN AND PRODUCED BY KRISSA ROSSBUND
PHOTOGRAPHY BY MARTY BALDWIN

¡Oh! Man

Design is going masculine—but no rough-around-the-edges man caves here! This style is decidedly debonair.

after years of looks that veered toward all things light and bright, the design industry is showing a little muscle, accelerating toward the intersection of masculine and sophisticated. This new direction is informed by design's mighty cousin, architecture—and its array of head-turning new details. Windows now boast sturdy steel frames, and millwork that has long been painted—usually white— now wears black. Wood has shed its painted layers for a natural look that celebrates beautiful grain. Fresh furniture and accessory pieces are joining the masculine movement. Sometimes tall, sometimes short, sometimes light, and sometimes dark, they're all handsome. Get ready to be swept off your feet.

BERNHARDT

CR Laine The "Brinkley" armchair flaunts leather with nailhead trim and a painted frame with turned knobs and tapered legs. **Mitchell Gold + Bob Williams** The "Woven Hide" pillow crisscrosses nutmeg-hue hides. **Artistica Home** The "Barito" table's nickel post links a snakeskin top and base. **Ralph Lauren Home** The brass casing of the "Brennan" clock rests on a leather base. The same leather accents the "Brennan" valet. **Blue Print** Onyx forms a lidded box. **Cerno** "Penna" oiled-walnut LED sconces feature brass accents. (*Preceding page*) **Jonathan Charles** Strong lines distinguish a "Geometric" wire-brushed oak chest. **Jayson Home** "Brass-Ridged" bowls reflect the striking base of the "Ursa" lamp. **Hancock & Moore** "Drake" bench in mottled "Lizard Bronze" leather. **Loloi** "Tess" throw. **Alexa Hampton for Theodore Alexander** Faceted "Penelope" accent table. **L'Objet** "Coba" stool with painted 18k gold accents. **York Wallcoverings** "Flapper" geometric wallpaper.

A.R.T Furniture The "Ellis" nightstand boasts tapered legs, brass hardware, and a travertine top. **Wildwood** The "White Creek" lamp sports driftwood strips and antique-bronze details while the "Fig" canister glimmers with an antique-bronze finish. **Jayson Home** The conical "Zinc Form" recalls models once used for drawing instruction. **Chelsea House** The "Alligator" box is tactile in faux alligator skin. **A.R.T Furniture** The bronze-tone linear base of the "Ennis" nightstand supports a shelf and storage drawer in gray undertones. **Palecek** White marble disks and antique-gold detail highlight the "Cora" lamp. **Ralph Lauren Home** The "Clermont" object references the form of Art Deco race cars. **Loloi** Indian-made pillows exude tribal influences. **Élitis** "Caissa" gridded wood wallcovering.

Wesley Hall The tufted leather "Webster" chair nods to a baseball glove. Mitchell Gold + Bob Williams "Brushstroke" pillow. Lee Industries A metal base contrasts the wheat-color chenille seat on the "1858" chair. Ambella Home The "Buckled" ottoman features a belted leather accent. Modern History The "Georgian" console offers rich tones from a fruitwood veneer. L'Objet "Han" black porcelain canisters and backgammon set made of Macassar ebony wood, marble, and shell inlay. Wildwood "Doric" fluted lamp and "Torso" figure. Chelsea House The "NY" drink table combines a mahogany base, black glass top, and antique-gold edging. Palecek "Scallop Shells" low metal bowl. Richard Mishaan for Theodore Alexander "Henning" side table and "Greenbrain" star chair. Fielding Archer Turned salvaged-wood candlesticks. Barclay Butera for Lexington "Lucca" ottoman in embossed zebra-print leather.

Taylor King The tubular brass-tone frame of the "Rice" chair offsets a gray-and-brown chenille fabric. **Ambella Home** A loose take on plaid, "Manuel Terrazzo" fabric covers the "Logan" chair. **Chelsea House** Gold-painted wood outlines the raffia-wrapped "Yangon" console table. A sinuous leopard figure crawls along its top. **Palecek** Coconut shell beads are bleached white or dyed black, then sewn to the metal frame of the "Sumba" urn. **Jayson Home** Bins to corral throw blankets, magazines, or logs are made of two shades of leather highlighted with white baseball stitching. **Loloi** The "Maya" throw weaves in an array of colors including hunter green, red, and butternut. **Arte** "Hover" nonwoven wallcovering depicts bronze-hue flying geese on a gray wood background. **Loloi** Rug fragments are framed and transformed into textural art.

Lee Industries "L3303" swivel armchair in Harness Black leather with contrasting cable-stitch closure. **Loloi** "Della" woven throw blanket in black and cream. **Caracole** The "Lofty" desk chair sports dark walnut legs, luxurious black velvet upholstery with a swirl design, and leather armrests that curve from the chair's back. **Aronson Woodworks** "C" accent table in "Horn" ombré finish over salvaged solid ash wood. **Alexa Hampton for Theodore Alexander** "Vlad" hexagon wall mirror with faceted mirror pieces. **Innovations** "Mazarin" wallcovering in Dresden, crafted of hand-applied cork and metallic foil, depicts a geometric pattern.

Mitchell Gold
+Bob Williams /30

THIRTY YEARS OF DESIGN AND INNOVATION

MGBWHOME.COM

Rising Stars of Design

The future of traditional design looks amazing—thanks to a fresh crop of designers shaping classical interiors for modern life. Meet our New Trad Class of 2019.

PRODUCED BY JENNY BRADLEY PFEFFER
WRITTEN BY SALLY FINDER WEEPIE

Ryan Saghian

We fell under the spell of this L.A. charmer when we set eyes on his über-luxe kitchen designs. (Yes, classic black and white look even better in the form of a goes-on-forever black marble backsplash.) Inspired by the high style of Dorothy Draper and Tony Duquette—and the rich patterns and colors of his Iranian heritage—Ryan reinterprets the glamour of Old Hollywood through a California modern lens. That vision? Definitely 20/20.

Brittany Bromley
When you grow up with Alessandra Branca as a close family friend, you're bound to speak fluent classicism. Brittany does—in today's fresh vernacular. The Chicago-born, Bedford, New York-based designer gets us. She knows we want a to-die-for traditional French bergère—covered in a performance bouclé wool that merely shrugs when wet bathing suits are headed its way.

Beata Heuman

Dare we call her a bit of a cheeky monkey? This London designer learned the biz from irrepressible icon Nicky Haslam. Now she's punching up traditional style with playful color and irreverent attitude—and we're bananas about the look.

PHOTOGRAPHY: BRITTANY BROMLEY ROOM, JANE BEILES; PORTRAIT, MARC TOUISSANT. BEATA HEUMAN ROOM AND PORTRAIT, SIMON BROWN. RYAN SAGHIAN ROOM ANTHONY BARCELO, PORTRAIT DANIEL SOFRANO

SOMETHING SPECIAL

Erik Peterson

Architectural details are our love language, and this Chicago native and Iowa State grad (go, Cyclones!), speaks it fluently. The principal of PHX Architecture, Erik took our breath away with his ability to artfully nestle a new Phoenix home amid the saguaros and with his light, sophisticated reinvention of Tuscan style. The former Taliesin Associated Architects intern is building a career that would make Frank Lloyd Wright proud.

Margaret Naeve Parker

We became obsessed with Margaret's style after visiting her chic shop, M Naeve, in Houston. Now we're just as taken with her timeless interiors—made irresistible with rich texture, muted color, and, of course, the exceptional antiques she uncovers on her travels.

Lindsey Coral Harper

"Get the scale and the furniture layout right, and you can pretty much do whatever you want colorwise," Lindsey says. She's made us believers. We're crushing on the lush, saturated palettes this Southern-born, New York-based designer conjures to put an unexpected edge into refined traditional rooms. Teal and persimmon? Lavender and Prussian blue? Chartreuse and navy? Yes, yes, and yes, please!

Laura Hodges

OK, we admit it. We have passport envy. This British-born, Washington, D.C.-based designer has traveled to more than 30 countries. It's no surprise that global influences are a hallmark of her tailored, classic rooms. "Exploring a different culture opens my mind to new ways of approaching design," the Jamie Drake/Thomas Jayne protégeé says. What will inspiration from her latest trip, to Cuba, yield? We can't wait to see.

ANDREW BROWN

Growing up in France and West Africa, this Birmingham, Alabama, designer contracted incurable wanderlust. His trips to Paris flea markets, Tokyo antique textile shops, and Cape Town art galleries inspire eclectic rooms that exude comfort. He loves "brown" furniture, plaster busts, and Palladian architecture. If there's Tinder for interior design, we swipe right.

Starrett Hoyt Ringbom

Happy, colorful, and just plain fun. That sums up Starrett—and her rooms. This fashion plate, based in New York, practically grew up in her mom's chic boutique, then honed her design skills under the eyes of Fernando Santangelo and Jonathan Adler. Now Starrett's cultured, daring, always-grounded-in-traditional style is turning heads. Ours included.

Mallory Mathison Glenn

We love how Mallory is putting a fresh face on Southern style. The Atlantan respects classic scale, fabrics, and furniture. (Bring on the Chinese Chippendale in droves!) But she's also adept at adding pop with color, pattern, and contemporary art. "I'd love to see a Rothko or Kandinsky hanging in Buckingham Palace," she says. Now *that's* New Trad.

"NEW TRADITIONAL IS ABOUT LIVING WITH WHAT YOU LOVE."

—designer Mallory Mathison Glenn

Q&a

Interior designer Michele Plachter
gives a Philadelphia warehouse condo
its declaration of inventiveness

WRITTEN BY KRISSA ROSSBUND
PHOTOGRAPHY BY ANDREA CIPRIANI MECCHI

Exterior Situated in the artist-charged Old City district of Philadelphia, dubbed the most historic square mile in America, the 1914 warehouse was converted into condos in 2002. It's part of a revamped neighborhood of galleries and American history.
Dining room Defined by original soaring windows that are graced with arched and circular muntins, the dining room was fitted with heirloom furniture from the client's mother. The varied wood tones, natural linen drapery panels, and crystal chandelier soften the black-and-ivory room.

Q What is the appeal of designing in a large warehouse space that originally had commercial purposes?

A I'm a city designer, so a space like this is a dream. The elevator shaft is always a feat, but once it opens, a glorious space unfolds. In this case, my client combined two condos, so the vantage point is stunning. The exposed ductwork and brick walls present a different kind of elegance that leaves cookie-cutter design behind.

Q How do you know when to update and when to leave original elements as they are?

A I have no tricks. It's a gut feeling. There's this idea that old means good. That's not always true. The dining chairs have beautiful shapes but needed a lift with an updated fabric. High-gloss black paint around the windows delivers luxury while maintaining urban grit. The grain of the existing wood gave soul to the room that I would never alter.

Tile inspired by wherever your passport takes you.

Inspiration isn't always obvious, but the right partner should be.
Order your complimentary samples and create your digital account
at CrossvilleInc.com.

Floor: **Gotham** | Wall: **Color by Numbers** | Counterton: **State of Grace** by Crossville

CROSSVILLE®
What Inspires You, Inspires Us.

Living room Establishing a modern attitude, the tailored silhouette of a new tufted sofa contrasts the raw quality of an organic bench. The armchairs are repurposed from the client's former home in New York. A cocktail table adds a touch of sheen among the textural arrangement that rests atop a thick shag carpet. **Bath** Dynamic photography ushers personal style into the bath, where a cast-iron tub sports a silver finish. **Master bedroom** A sleigh bed sets the color tone, repeating on an old chest of drawers and an armoire. A tufted bench, crystal chandelier, and shag rug enhance the lightness of the room's foundation of painted brick walls and pleated linen draperies that span the large windows.

Q "Brown wood" furniture that's been abandoned in design for so long adds charm to the bedroom. How did you make the traditional furniture current and work within an industrial setting?

A People miss history and are looking for comfort in pieces that tell a story. The wood furniture that my client inherited accomplished that. I added surprise with a new sparkling chandelier to imply sophistication. The white-painted brick walls and a modern bench give the space balance instead of an old, dated feeling.

Q This condo seemingly emphasizes texture and layering over bold color. But color shows up in the artwork. Why here?

A These sorts of industrial spaces commonly walk down the path of sleek, contemporary design in black and white, but I aimed for glamorous and warm. My client's colorful artwork grabs attention in the living room, which is an eclectic mix of classic and modern, hard and soft, shiny and raw. Art has power, and it speaks to the personality of its owner. The goal is always to create a home that is unique. ⊞

PHOTOGRAPH: LIVING ROOM, KIP DAWKINS

DELTA®
VOICEIQ™
TECHNOLOGY

It's Prismatic

Faceted forms plus canted corners and geometric prints equals undeniably attractive dimension in furniture, fabrics, and accessories

WRITTEN AND PRODUCED BY CLARA HANEBERG   PHOTOGRAPHY BY MARTY BALDWIN

Clé Go 3-D with "Fornace Brioni Mantegna" concrete wall tiles (*cletile.com*). **Designers Guild** Fluid "Bougival" fabric in cobalt plays well indoors and out (*designersguild.com*). **Maharam** "Arcade" fabric features a modern geometric motif (*maharam.com*). **Currey & Company** Inspired by mosaic tile patterns, the "Leiden" nightstand employs different veneers for a play on light and dark (*curreyandcompany.com*). **Relativity Textiles** Screen-printed by hand in Chicago, "Escher" wallcovering exudes graphic appeal in gold and silver (*relativitytextiles.com*). **Kelly Wearstler for Lee Jofa** "Covet" wallcovering in Denim lives up to its name, flaunting an irresistible faceted motif (*kravet.com*). **CB2** "Magma Metal" nesting tables dazzle with finishes of warm bronze, burnt bronze, and dark silver plate (*cb2.com*). **Arteriors** Spiked with perforations, the "Tyson" pendant plays all the angles (*arteriorshome.com*). **Barbara Barry for Baker** The "Prism" table lamp intrigues with a sculptural ceramic base (*bakerfurniture.com*). **Mitchell Gold + Bob Williams** Evoking a gemstone, the "Jewel" swivel chair sports jade velvet (*mgbwhome.com*). **Theodore Alexander** "Diamond Cut" vases make a distressed finish stately (*theodorealexander.com*). **Global Views** Give flowers a new spin in the "Prism" vase (*globalviews.com*). ⊞

Shift Your Outlook.

[8:15 am]

[10:00 am]

California King

Pacific Design Center showroom luminary Thomas Lavin reigns over a life well-balanced and well-lived

WRITTEN AND PRODUCED BY KRISSA ROSSBUND
PHOTOGRAPHY BY MICHAEL GARLAND

Thomas Lavin turns to the expertise of his sister, Mary Tostado, and mom, Fyfe Lavin, to make his operation sing. He's always on top of the latest furniture releases, meeting with makers like Jiun Ho.

The sheer size of Los Angeles' Pacific Design Center makes it feel like a modern-day palace, minus the intricate scrolls and gilding. Much like the grand homes of royals, the building is divided into moments of individual style—and Thomas Lavin's almost 20-year-old showroom puts him in line to claim the longevity throne.

With a modern slant to lighting and furniture, the showroom, newly expanded by 4,000 square feet to include the country's sole noncorporate Christian Liaigre boutique, also unfurls a wealth of fabric options that range from classic and traditional to contemporary.

Whether he's imagining striking vistas within the showroom or picturing his newest arts endeavor, Thomas has a grand day in store. Come along as we follow him through a few hours in L.A.

[10:30 am]

[11:30 am]

[noon]

> "MY ENGAGEMENT IN THE BUSINESS IS DRIVEN BY MY CURIOSITY TO KEEP LEARNING." —Thomas Lavin

[5:30 am] Thomas doesn't wait for the sun to rise in Los Angeles. He's up with the East Coast dwellers. A routine of Pilates or yoga at the gym followed by a cup of green tea jump-starts a day that promises a rich roster of activity.

[8:15 am] So many folks say goodbye to family as they begin their professional workdays. But when Thomas arrives at his showroom, he's saying hello. His sister, Mary Tostado, plays "drill master," assisting Thomas with sales meetings, setting goals for sales representatives, and fostering client relations. In Thomas' expansive inventory of textiles and wallcoverings, mother knows best. Fyfe Lavin shepherds products into display masterpieces in the showroom. Thomas meets with them and his staff to start the morning, then works on his own ideas for new floor plans.

[10:00 am] Thomas and furniture maker Jiun Ho have grown up together in the design industry, launching their businesses in 2000.

Their childhoods, though, are a different story. Thomas is a Los Angeles native, while Jiun hails from Malaysia. When Jiun visits from his San Francisco headquarters, the pair share their global experiences in conversations that delve into the heart of furniture design.

[10:30 am] After a chat with a fellow creative, the lightbulbs are going off. From a perch in the showroom's lighting gallery, Thomas takes time to put down ideas.

[11:30 am] Time to wrap up today's work in the showroom and shift gears to off-campus activity.

[noon] First up, lunch! Thomas meets with close friend and designer Matt O'Dorisio at nearby Lucques, a refined restaurant acclaimed for its market-driven California cuisine—and owned by former *Traditional Home* resident chef Suzanne Goin. You realize Thomas is a regular when you spot TL Veggies on the menu. The tasty assembly of seasonal vegetables was named in his honor.

Adatto™ Bath
with Mincio™ Filler

BEST. DECISION. EVER.

For projects of any size, perfection often requires making difficult decisions. Allow the experts at Ferguson to make things easy by introducing you to an extensive collection of stylish products from prominent brands, all designed to bring your vision to life. Learn more at **fergusonshowrooms.com**

✦ FERGUSON
Bath, Kitchen & Lighting Gallery

[2:00 pm]

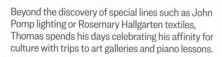
Beyond the discovery of special lines such as John Pomp lighting or Rosemary Hallgarten textiles, Thomas spends his days celebrating his affinity for culture with trips to art galleries and piano lessons.

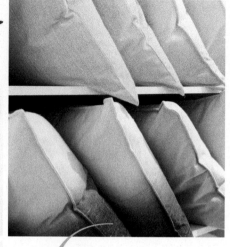

[7:00 pm]

[5:30 pm]

THERE'S NOTHING THAT I WON'T DO. I HAVEN'T LOST THE PASSION."

—Thomas Lavin

[2:00 pm] To deepen relationships with industry creatives—and satisfy his appetite for new design and art, Thomas takes time to visit studios. He's a frequent visitor to Los Angeles' Edward Cella galleries, where he's introduced to works that he brings to his showroom. Today, works by contemporary artist Ruth Pastine, who paints with simplicity in intense color, catch his eye.

[5:30 pm] For Thomas, a life rich with culture embraces all the senses. Piano music audibly decorates his Hollywood Hills home with timeless beauty. His musical inclinations are inherited from his great-grandmother, whose living room was anchored by a Steinway grand piano. Childhood interest and lessons blossomed into a classical piano performance major during college at UCLA. But life on campus proved that while Thomas was passionate about the piano as a hobby, he didn't want to make a career of it. But he still

indulges in piano lessons once a week after work, and a 1940 Steinway holds a spot of honor in his abode. "I practice whenever I can because I know that the teacher is coming," he says. "I'm currently working on a Beethoven sonata. And my boyfriend, Destin Bass, sings, so we like to perform for family and friends."

[7:00 pm] After the final music chord has faded and the sun begins to melt into the horizon, it's time for Thomas to wind down. As he channels his bartending proficiency with a "wildly cold and up with onions" martini, he sports a traditional silk ikat caftan that he purchased on a trip to Morocco. The evening is augmented with whiffs of Israeli food—he and Destin are working to master the cuisine of Israeli-English chef Yotam Ottolenghi.

[8:00 pm] A movie or a book? Thomas caps his night with both. A 1980s French New Wave film titled *Diva* is cued on his television, and F. Scott Fitzgerald's *Tender Is the Night* rests on his bedside table. Some treasured moments, then lights out.

Always learning, always pursuing the best culture has to offer— that's how Thomas Lavin chooses to live. And tomorrow he'll do it all again.

FEATURED TILE: MILAS LILAC MARBLE

#THETILESHOP

FASHION, MEET FUNCTION

SCHEDULE A COMPLIMENTARY CONSULTATION
AND DESIGN YOUR DREAM ROOM AT ONE OF
OUR 140 SHOWROOMS OR TILESHOP.COM/TH

The Tile Shop

New Threads

What's the stitch? Today's needlework shows off modern graphic designs and gotta-feel-it dimension while furthering the fabric of artisans past.

WRITTEN AND PRODUCED BY CLARA HANEBERG   PHOTOGRAPHY BY MARTY BALDWIN

> I INTEGRATE EMBROIDERY LIKE I WOULD A PRINTED FABRIC. IT'S NOSTALGIC AND LUXURIOUS."
> —designer Rachel Cannon

Stitch this on your folk art sampler: Embroidery is in. The new-age needlepoint scene is bright and bursting with talented artisans and elevated textile treatments. While speaking the language of the Instagram age, these iterations nod to the traditional art, which has been around as long as humans have put thread to fabric. Elaborately embroidered items have been a mark of status in many cultures including ancient Persia, India, and China, and medieval and Baroque Europe. Today's striking designs could cause history to repeat itself. So grab a needle—let's thread! ⊞

Taylor King The "Cheswick" wing chair sports "Santorino" embroidered linen fabric (*taylorking.com*). **Samuel & Sons** Ensure your draperies and sofa skirts are well-trimmed with "Mireille" and "Corinne" embroidered borders (*samuelandsons.com*). **Marigold Living** The "Florentina" tablecloth was inspired by the stitching of founder Shreya Shah's mother (*marigoldliving.com*). **Janet Gregg** The pink "Geometric" and neutral "Pucci" needlepoint pillows are made to order (*janetgregg.com*). **Francesca Colussi Cramer** Vintage postcards are hand-embroidered by the British textile artist (*colussicramer.bigcartel.com*). **Hibiscus Linens** Let embroidered "Topiary" dinner napkins bring lush greenery to your tablescape (*hibiscuslinens.com*). **Lycette Designs** Founder Jessica Chaney reimagines traditional needlework through a millennial lens on the cheeky "Crocodile" canvas (*lycettedesigns.com*).

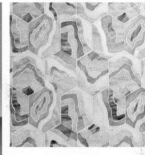

Fearless Flair

Big, bold pattern on wallpaper is a trend and a tradition. Pair chartreuse-tinged greens with hits of teal and pink to balance a classic motif with contemporary attitude.

PRODUCED BY JENNY BRADLEY PFEFFER   PHOTOGRAPHY BY JEAN ALLSOPP

Sherwin-Williams "Verdant"

Behr "Plumage"

Farrow & Ball "Pitch Black"

PPG "Floral Linen"

Every space needs a bit of breathing room. But that doesn't necessarily mean swaths of white. Designers Courtney Coleman and Bill Brockschmidt used a different strategy in this dining room: audacious color.

"We wanted to contrast the exotic 19th-century wallpaper with a bold piece of contemporary art to breathe air into the saturated space," Brockschmidt says.

The simple, abstract forms of the painting calm the busy, regular pattern of the paper. Rather than distracting from the room's flow, the contrast brings cohesiveness—thanks to the designers' decision to layer in unifying elements.

"The colors and forms of the lamp and the urn," Brockschmidt explains, "very subtly bring harmony to the intentional juxtaposition of the dominant wallpaper and painting." The bold becomes beautiful. ⊞

Williamsburg®

BRING HISTORY HOME

Our nation's colonial period shaped an enduring tradition in architectural design. Benjamin Moore used research from Colonial Williamsburg preservationists to create the Williamsburg® Paint Color Collection, a timeless palette of 144 beautifully nuanced colors that bring a celebration of American heritage to traditional and contemporary architecture.

*Visit BenjaminMoore.com/Williamsburg
for more information.*

Benjamin Moore®

Paint like no other.®

Tried, Trad & TRUE

Traditional Home and Benjamin Moore check in with 2018 New Trad Dan Mazzarini of BHDM Design to find out what surprising shade makes a bedroom feel cozy no matter what the season.

Benjamin Moore
Mediterranean Olive
2142-10

Photography by Adam Macchia

MEDITERRANEAN INSPIRATION "Deep shades make a bedroom feel cocoon-like, and in this space, I chose Benjamin Moore's Mediterranean Olive. This can be a bold choice for a bedroom, but it reads as a calming neutral with the right décor. Here I brought in earthy furnishings like this woven headboard and ceramic lamp to give the room a sanctuary, spa-like vibe. I find that deeper tones wrap a room in warmth, and this is why paint quality and coverage are so important. With Benjamin Moore's Gennex® color technology, you will get remarkable color saturation and accuracy, which are absolutely worth the investment."

To see more of Dan's work visit **www.BHDMdesign.com** or **@danmazzarini** on Instagram

Benjamin Moore®

www.benjaminmoore.com

UNMATCHABLE

When you find the perfect color, **nothing else will do.**
Perfection comes from our paint and our proprietary Gennex®
colorants, together, creating results that are breathtaking.
Rely on Benjamin Moore for premium quality and
Gennex Color Technology, which makes our
long-lasting colors, all 3,500 of them, one-of-a-kind.
Unmatchable.

WALL: *Stormy Monday*
2112-50, Aura® Eggshell

Benjamin Moore®

THE ART OF THE PATIO

BUILT TO OUTCOMFORT & OVERLAST | WOODARD-FURNITURE.COM

Woodard™

life & style

PHOTOGRAPH BY NATHAN SCHRODER

LIFE AS ART

Collected pieces make life more beautiful, telling the stories of our travels, tracing the history of our family, or in the case of this copperware, inspiring an exquisite kitchen and equally enticing meals. Feed your kitchen daydreams in "French Connection," page 57.

Show your true colors.
ALL OF THEM.

DACORMATCH

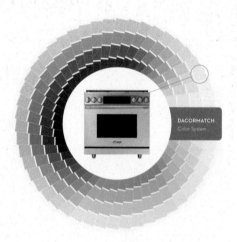

Personalize your appliances
in any color imaginable.
Make it your own.

NEW YORK | CHICAGO | LOS ANGELES

French Connection

A Dallas kitchen speaks to a love of France—its architecture, artisans, and culinary delights

WRITTEN BY SALLY FINDER WEEPIE   PHOTOGRAPHY BY NATHAN SCHRODER   PRODUCED BY JENNY O'CONNOR

> # "EVERYTHING HAS A PATINA."
> —designer
> Heidi Arwine

Food is the language of love, they say, and in this house, all that amour has a distinctly French accent.

It's influenced by the formal French-style exterior of the Dallas home—and by the Francophiles who live here. "She loves French architecture, cooking, and baking," interior designer Heidi Arwine says. "And she had dreamed of having a La Cornue range. So that was the first order of business—getting the La Cornue ordered."

But Arwine, who worked in tandem with architect Christy Blumenfeld on the project, didn't stop there. She and Blumenfeld gave the family a complete La Cornue kitchen with base cabinets that echo the elegance of the copper-trimmed range.

The copper story continues on the trim decorating the custom vent hood and on cookware that fills ceiling-mounted shelves. "The homeowner already owned all of that copper," Arwine says. "We created the shelves to showcase the pieces that she loves."

Arwine and Blumenfeld designed the shelves—statement makers in their own right—to work in harmony with new windows. Each shelf aligns perfectly with a muntin to ensure uninterrupted sight lines and light that flows beautifully.

The windows—one on each side of the range hood—were one of Blumenfeld's big moves during the renovation. The kitchen needed natural light, but Blumenfeld was hesitant to alter the original architecture created by Richard Drummond Davis—until she found Davis' plans and discovered that the windows were supposed to be there all along. "That was our green light," Arwine says.

Blumenfeld also switched out a coffered ceiling in favor of exposed beams that add to the kitchen's rustic French aesthetic. The dark tones of the beams jibe with cabinetry, including an artisan-made dish pantry outfitted with contrasting natural wood doors with metal mesh inserts.

"Everything has a patina," Arwine says. The table base is an antique lathe from Europe. Its graceful, timeworn form acts as counterpoint to new marble that will soon, too, wear history on its surface.

Baking kitchen The refrigerator looks like an old-time icebox, but it's actually a new pro-grade unit from Sub-Zero. Shelves with abundant lighting hold all of the homeowner's baking essentials. **Preceding page** French flair reverberates through the kitchen with a La Cornue range and lavish use of marble, including ledges ingeniously built into the backsplash. Pendants from Visual Comfort add an industrial edge.

**Redefining Surfaces.
Redefining Kitchens.**

DEKTON®
designed by COSENTINO

Kitchens evolve, they become social
spaces in which we do not only cook, but
live in.We have created a resistant and
durable material with unlimited designs,
to create all sorts of spaces.

A product designed by COSENTINO®

Flooring color **Dekton Lunar**
Kitchen Island **Dekton Bergen**

Find out more about the **25-year transferable Dekton warranty,**
look out inspiration and find resources at **cosentino.com**

Cosentino North America 355 Alhambra Cir Suite 1000, Coral Gables, FL 33134 - (786) 686-5060   f 🐦 📷 @CosentinoUSA

"Marble countertops are a huge part of the French kitchen," Arwine says. "The homeowner didn't want to sacrifice that to worries that it would stain. She loves that it will tell the story of her family."

That story will include many chapters of whipping up delectable treats in the adjacent butler's pantry/second kitchen, a dream space for a homeowner who "takes baking to new level," Blumenfeld says.

Here, the push and pull of the palette shifts black to a supporting role on Via Lactea granite countertops and spotlights white on cabinetry and panels that cloak a refrigerator and freezer. Custom hardware gives the look of an old-fashioned icebox.

"The family bakes together, eats together, and hangs out together here—that's why I love this kitchen," Blumenfeld says. "It brings them together in a really special way." 🏠

Interior designer: Heidi Arwine **Architect:** Christy Blumenfeld

For more information, see sources on page 118

Kitchen Custom ceiling-mounted shelving hangs above a Waterstone faucet. Artisans at Seal Tex Metals in Dallas fabricated the shelf units and the vent hood cover. Marble counters look seamless, but they hide pop-up outlets. Collected pieces—including the homeowner's cookware and dishes—give the kitchen character, patina, and a sense of history.

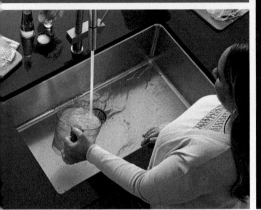

Sweet Beginnings

Maple syrup and other tempting fall flavors are on the menu at this brunch, where the table is set with fresh blue-and-white ceramics

WRITTEN AND PRODUCED BY KRISSA ROSSBUND   PHOTOGRAPHY BY BLAINE MOATS

autumn, how sweet you are! Cool, crisp weather piques the appetite and transforms maple leaves into dazzling red, orange, and gold. Celebrate this glorious season with a brunch that highlights another of the maple tree's sweet gifts—maple syrup—and a host of fall favorites, including butternut squash, pears, and apple cider.

To complement the tempting menu and make the meal even more memorable, set the table with a collection of new ceramics from global arbiter of good taste Ralph Lauren. The color scheme—beloved blue and white—isn't unusual, but the collection's intriguing patterns and history are.

In creating the ceramics, designers for Ralph Lauren Home—a brand that represents classic American style—looked across the pond to England's Burleigh, maker of earthenware since 1851. The pieces marry timelessness and ➤

A creamy ivory dining room serves as a classic canvas for an equally classic tabletop. The chandelier is from Circa Lighting.

A collaboration between Ralph Lauren Home and Burleigh has produced a new earthenware collection steeped in classic patterns. Here, the "Faded Peony" serving platter presents waffles and eggs topped with maple syrup-glazed prosciutto while the "Midnight Sky" platter adds star quality to an arugula, pear, walnut, and Parmesan salad. Maple syrup and sea salt finish Butternut Squash Gougères with a sweet and savory bite.

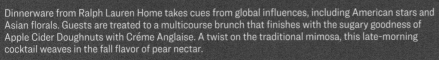

Dinnerware from Ralph Lauren Home takes cues from global influences, including American stars and Asian florals. Guests are treated to a multicourse brunch that finishes with the sugary goodness of Apple Cider Doughnuts with Créme Anglaise. A twist on the traditional mimosa, this late-morning cocktail weaves in the fall flavor of pear nectar.

Ralph Lauren Home's silver-plated chargers and "Kings" flatware hint at glamour and contrast the indigo "Seto Texture" tablecloth. Flowers in a fall palette complement the array of blues. Petite waffles keep the multicourse brunch light and energizing.

luxury as they offer takes on two motifs: graphic stars and flowing florals.

The florals—one with a loose vine design and another that layers faded peonies for a saturated presentation—take inspiration from East Asian hand-blocked batik prints. Finished by hand, the versatile dinnerware is enhanced by a mix of materials including clear crystal and silver—and showcased by textural indigo tablecloth fabric.

Fiery colors on centerpiece florals complement the blue table setting as they evoke the colors of maple leaves and nod to the tree's other tasteful contribution to the menu—the syrup that adds a dazzling finish to butternut squash gougères, layers a complex note into an arugula salad, and brings a delightful surprise to luscious waffle batter. Autumn, you are sweet indeed. 🍴

menu

Fall Pear-Orange Mimosa

Butternut Squash Gougères

Arugula Salad with Pancetta,
Pear, and Walnuts

Scrambled Egg, Prosciutto, and
Mascarpone-Topped Waffles

Apple Cider Doughnuts with
Créme Anglaise

MENU AND RECIPES BY
CHEF MARY PAYNE MORAN

For recipes and a shopping list,
visit TraditionalHome.com/Maple

Open the Door
TO A TREATMENT FOR MODERATE TO SEVERE PAINFUL INTERCOURSE AFTER MENOPAUSE.

PAY AS LITTLE AS $15*
Good for up to 2 prescription fills of Premarin Vaginal Cream

Premarin® Rx only
(conjugated estrogens)
vaginal cream

Prescription Premarin Vaginal Cream is clinically proven to relieve moderate to severe painful intercourse caused by menopausal changes, which affects a surprising number of women. Unlike over-the-counter treatments, it delivers estrogens directly to the source of the pain. It helps rebuild vaginal tissue and make intercourse more comfortable.

So open the conversation. Talk to your doctor about Premarin Vaginal Cream today.

Learn more at www.PremarinVaginalCream.com/Savings

IMPORTANT SAFETY INFORMATION AND INDICATIONS

Using estrogen-alone may increase your chance of getting cancer of the uterus (womb). Report any unusual vaginal bleeding right away while you are using Premarin (conjugated estrogens) Vaginal Cream. Vaginal bleeding after menopause may be a warning sign of cancer of the uterus (womb). Your healthcare provider should check any unusual vaginal bleeding to find out the cause.

Do not use estrogens, with or without progestins, to prevent heart disease, heart attacks, strokes or dementia (decline in brain function).

Using estrogen-alone may increase your chances of getting strokes or blood clots. Using estrogens with progestins may increase your chances of getting heart attacks, strokes, breast cancer, or blood clots.

Using estrogens, with or without progestins, may increase your chance of getting dementia, based on a study of women 65 years of age or older.

Estrogens should be used at the lowest dose possible, only for as long as needed. You and your healthcare provider should talk regularly about whether you still need treatment.

Premarin (conjugated estrogens) Vaginal Cream should not be used if you have unusual vaginal bleeding, have or had cancer, had a stroke or heart attack, have or had blood clots or liver problems, have a bleeding disorder, are allergic to any of its ingredients, or think you may be pregnant.

Estrogens increase the risk of gallbladder disease. Discontinue estrogen if loss of vision, pancreatitis, or liver problems occur. If you take thyroid medication, consult your healthcare provider, as use of estrogens may change the amount needed.

Common side effects include headache, pelvic pain, breast pain, vaginal bleeding and vaginitis.

INDICATIONS

Premarin (conjugated estrogens) Vaginal Cream is used after menopause to treat menopausal changes in and around the vagina and to treat moderate to severe painful intercourse caused by these changes.

Each gram contains 0.625 mg of conjugated estrogens, USP.

Please see Important Product Information on the next page.

You may report any issues related to Pfizer products by calling Pfizer at 1-800-438-1985 (US only). Or if you prefer, you may contact the FDA directly: please visit www.fda.gov/MedWatch, or call 1-800-FDA-1088.

IMPORTANT FACTS Premarin®
(conjugated estrogens) (prem-uh-rin)
vaginal cream

ABOUT PREMARIN® VAGINAL CREAM

PREMARIN Vaginal Cream is a medicine that contains a mixture of estrogen hormones. PREMARIN Vaginal Cream is used after menopause to treat menopausal changes in and around the vagina and painful intercourse caused by these changes. You and your healthcare provider should talk regularly about whether you still need treatment with PREMARIN Vaginal Cream.

IMPORTANT SAFETY INFORMATION

What is the most important information I should know about PREMARIN Vaginal Cream (an estrogen mixture)?

- Using estrogen-alone may increase your chance of getting cancer of the uterus (womb). Report any unusual vaginal bleeding right away while you are using PREMARIN Vaginal Cream. Vaginal bleeding after menopause may be a warning sign of cancer of the uterus (womb). Your healthcare provider should check any unusual vaginal bleeding to find the cause.
- Do not use estrogen-alone or estrogens with progestin to prevent heart disease, heart attacks, strokes or dementia (decline in brain function).
- Using estrogen-alone may increase your chances of getting strokes or blood clots.
- Using estrogen with progestins may increase your chances of getting heart attacks, strokes, breast cancer, or blood clots.
- Using estrogen-alone or combined with progestin may increase your chance of getting dementia, based on a study of women age 65 years or older.
- You and your healthcare provider should talk regularly about whether you still need treatment with PREMARIN Vaginal Cream.

DO NOT START USING PREMARIN VAGINAL CREAM IF YOU:

- Have unusual vaginal bleeding
- Currently have or have had certain cancers. Estrogens may increase the chance of getting certain types of cancers, including cancer of the breast or uterus. If you have or have had cancer, talk with your healthcare provider about whether you should use PREMARIN Vaginal Cream.
- Had a stroke or heart attack
- Currently have or have had blood clots
- Currently have or have had liver problems
- Have been diagnosed with a bleeding disorder
- Are allergic to PREMARIN Vaginal Cream or any of its ingredients
- Think you may be pregnant

Tell your healthcare provider:

- If you have any unusual vaginal bleeding
- About all your medical problems
- About all the medicines you take
- If you are going to have surgery or will be on bedrest
- If you are breast-feeding

POSSIBLE SIDE EFFECTS OF PREMARIN VAGINAL CREAM

PREMARIN Vaginal Cream is only used in and around the vagina; however, the risks associated with oral estrogens should be taken into account. Serious, but less common side effects include:

- Heart attack • Stroke • Blood clots • Dementia • Breast cancer
- Cancer of the uterus • Ovarian cancer • High blood pressure
- High blood sugar • Gallbladder disease • Liver problems
- Enlargement of benign tumors of the uterus • Severe allergic reaction

Call your healthcare provider right away if you get any of the following warning signs, or any other unusual symptoms that concern you:

- New breast lumps • Unusual vaginal bleeding
- Changes in speech or vision • Sudden new severe headaches
- Severe pains in your chest or legs with or without shortness of breath, weakness and fatigue • Swollen lips, tongue or face

Less serious, but common, side effects include:

- Headache • Breast pain • Irregular vaginal bleeding or spotting
- Stomach/abdominal cramps, bloating • Nausea and vomiting
- Hair loss • Fluid retention • Vaginal yeast infection • Reactions from inserting PREMARIN Vaginal Cream, such as vaginal burning, irritation, and itching

These are not all the possible side effects of PREMARIN Vaginal Cream. For more information, ask your healthcare provider or pharmacist for advice about side effects. You may report side effects to Pfizer Inc at 1-800-438-1985 or to the FDA at 1-800-FDA-1088.

HOW TO USE PREMARIN VAGINAL CREAM

PREMARIN Vaginal Cream is a cream that you place in your vagina with the applicator provided with the cream.

- Take the dose recommended by your healthcare provider and talk to him or her about how well that dose is working for you.
- You and your healthcare provider should talk regularly (for example, every 3 to 6 months) about the dose you are taking and whether you still need treatment with PREMARIN Vaginal Cream.

1. Remove cap from tube.
2. Screw nozzle end of applicator onto tube.
3. Gently squeeze tube from the bottom to force sufficient cream into the barrel to provide the prescribed dose. Use the marked stopping points on the applicator to measure the correct dose, as prescribed by your healthcare provider.
4. Unscrew applicator from tube.
5. Lie on back with knees drawn up. To deliver medication, gently insert applicator deeply into vagina and press plunger downward to its original position.
6. To cleanse: Pull plunger to remove it from barrel. Wash with mild soap and warm water. Do not boil or use hot water.

NEED MORE INFORMATION?

- This information does not replace talking to your healthcare provider about your menopausal symptoms and their treatment.
- Go to www.premarinvaginalcream.com
- Call **1-888-9-PREMARIN (1-888-977-3627).**

Distributed by

 Wyeth Pharmaceuticals Inc
A subsidiary of Pfizer Inc, Philadelphia, PA 19101

©2018 Pfizer Inc. All rights reserved. February 2018

COMBINE
HOME & AUTO

—

Feel good knowing you have the home and car insurance policies you deserve. You could even get a Multi-Policy discount.

GEICO®

geico.com | 1-800-947-AUTO (2886) | Local Agent

GARDEN
GLEN GARDNER

CHARLESTON
IN CHARGE

WRITTEN BY SALLY FINDER WEEPIE &
CLARA HANEBERG WITH TARA LARSON
PHOTOGRAPHY BY KATIE CHARLOTTE FIEDLER
PRODUCED BY JENNY BRADLEY PFEFFER

Fresh twists on traditional looks rule the day at our 2018 Southern Style Now Designer Showhouse in historic Charleston, presented in concert with Robert Leleux. Join us for an unforgettable amble through this reimagined 1840s Greek Revival home filled with spaces revitalized for modern living. We promise endless inspiration from more than a dozen talented designers— served with a great big helping of inimitable Southern charm.

CARRIAGE HOUSE DEN
TRACI ZELLER

PARLOR
MATTHEW CARTER

Carriage House Den Inspired by garden views and Southerners' love of color, Charlotte designer Traci Zeller crafted a pretty-as-a-party-dress palette for the carriage house den. Shades of brown, from camel to chocolate, meld with grassy green, fuchsia, and pale pink—including a ceiling swathed in Benjamin Moore's "Strawberry Yogurt." Textures—nubby chenille, natural linen, and soft velvet—make the mix even headier. An array of furnishings from CR Laine ensures the den is a perfect place for casual gatherings—or relaxation. "Because I can't think of anything dreamier than taking a nap in the sun *and* the air-conditioning, the niche had to have a daybed," Zeller says. When curling up with a good book is on the agenda, a floor lamp from Circa Lighting stands at the ready.

Parlor "I wanted the parlor to feel like Charleston, but in an unexpected way," Lexington, Kentucky, designer Matthew Carter says. "I loved the idea of really beautiful antique furniture mixed with more casual fabrics, like the small print on the linen curtains, then setting everything on fire with a really acidic and intense wall color: Benjamin Moore's 'Chartreuse.'" A thoughtful assemblage of furniture pieces in bright, fresh upholstery encourages hours of convivial conversation by the fire.

Entry & Stair Tower "I love the idea of big impact in a tiny space," designer Lindsey Coral Harper says. That's what the Georgia native achieved using a custom wallcovering from Gracie Studio. "The amazing poppy color and giant 3-foot-tall peonies work with a collection of art to create an unforgettable moment when you walk in. You're drawn up the staircase because you want to see the next gallery wall of original artwork." In all, she hung 100 pieces of art and a smattering of gilded sunburst mirrors along the three flights of stairs. Gray tones on some walls, the stair runner, and window treatments balance the energetic colors while a hanging fixture from Circa Lighting echoes the golden glow of frames, mirrors, and accessories.

Garden (page 70) History and modernity, graciousness and ease mingle in the verdant garden, designed by Charlestonian Glen Gardner. "The house itself is a very traditional Charleston single house with a fresh new rear window wall looking out to the garden," he says. "I wanted to allow the garden to speak to the house, which meant creating classic lines and timeless spaces with a fresh interpretation." He crafted a structured yet informal layout featuring a series of garden rooms. Surfaces shift from Crossville pavers to compacted gravel, yet each space is connected by a border of handmade brick and an organic green-and-white palette. A backdrop of lush yews is punctuated by pops of pink sasanqua camellia and yellow cassia. Primarily white-painted furniture pieces include a 1930s Leinfelder iron table that sits at the heart of the dining area. Lanterns from Bevolo Gas & Electric Lights let the party continue long after sunset.

ENTRY &
STAIR TOWER
**LINDSEY CORAL
HARPER**

Dining Room "I looked to Southern style past for inspiration," Raleigh designer MA Allen says, "and took cues from icons such as Colefax and Fowler, Billy Baldwin, William Haines, and Frances Elkins in designing the dining room." A hand-painted wallpaper from Gracie Studio provides a historical feel that meshes with architectural details—including ornate crown molding and a handsome fireplace—and recalls the palm-spiked Charleston landscape. Its neutral sepia tones also provide the perfect backdrop for explosive color in modern art, notably *A Gathering of Monarchs,* a mixed-media piece by Louis St. Lewis and Nate Sheaffer. Fabric on host chairs from Chaddock visually links the new pieces with vintage Maison Jansen side chairs. A three-tier brass chandelier with quartz accents by Kelly Wearstler for Circa Lighting cascades above the Chaddock dining table. "The formal Southern table is set for entertaining," Allen says, "but the unexpected layering of mixed china patterns and hues lends a playful and relaxed feel." China and silver are from Replacements, Ltd.

ELEVATED design

Designed to empower your most ambitious culinary endeavors, our newly redesigned Masterpiece® and Professional Collections combine unparalleled performance with leading innovation to tell two unique design stories. Elevate your cooking, without compromising your style.

See both collections at:
THERMADOR.COM

for EXPERIENCE
every

Featuring the PROFESSIONAL COLLECTION

Choosing
Exceptional
Appliances

Presented by **Thermador**

Today, who isn't fascinated with food? We dish on the hottest cooking shows, scour the farmers market for delectable produce, Instagram our culinary masterpieces—and serve them to rave reviews from family and friends. This is the Food Age, and the home chef needs exceptional appliances. That's where Thermador comes in, delivering professional results in this showhouse and in your kitchen. The standard cabinet-depth "Pro Harmony" six-burner gas range boasts powerful patented Star Burners for better searing and faster boiling. An ExtraLow® setting is perfect for simmering delicate sauces or keeping food warm without scorching or stirring. A roomy oven manages multiple dishes—and offers Full Access® telescopic racks with easy-grip handles that make it easy to wrangle heavy cookware. So set the table—dining excitement is on the way.

KITCHEN &
BUTLER'S
PANTRY
**MICHAEL
MITCHELL
AND TYLER
HILL**

WE WATCHED EVERY EPISODE
OF *DOWNTON ABBEY* AND
BECAME INSPIRED." —designer Michael Mitchell

Kitchen & Butler's Pantry Charleston-based designers Michael Mitchell and Tyler Hill of Mitchell Hill wanted the kitchen to feel modern and sophisticated while referencing the home's origins—and the designers' love of period glamour. "We watched every episode of *Downton Abbey* and became inspired by the characters, where they live, their lifestyle, and their fashion," Mitchell says. "This kitchen is the marriage of an 1840s paneled library and the 1940s machine age."

Paneled walls and classic cabinetry coated in Benjamin Moore's "Tavern Gray" serve as a timeless foil to an art-glass-meets-industrial ceiling that nods to midcentury artisanship. A dark brushed-steel framework holds mirrored

and aged-brass triangles that send light dancing throughout the room. "The mix of glass and metals has always been a personal signature of ours," Hill says. "There's something special about how the two elements play together."

A masculine palette of olive and sand balances the powerful color seen in the home's other rooms. Soapstone countertops with olive veining expand on the hues of blackened metal while stainless-steel appliances repeat the shimmer of mirrored surfaces. A six-burner Thermador range establishes a pro-grade chef's station under a custom mirrored ventilation hood. A DXV pot-filler faucet in polished chrome set on a wall of sandy-hue Yin + Yang collection

backsplash tile from Crossville provides convenience for the cook.

A striking photograph by Aldara Ortega hangs over the primary sink, making dishwashing duty almost as pleasant as a visit to the art gallery. Lighting controls by Lutron ensure it's easy to adjust the mood. An island with bar stool seating encourages guests to gather around and help with the cooking. Emtek hardware in satin brass and a vintage French clock continue the metal medley started by the custom ceiling.

Subtle sparkle continues in the adjacent butler's pantry, outfitted with glass shelves set against a recessed mirror. A Thermador wine refrigerator keeps favorite vintages at hand.

Master Bedroom "I was born in the South, and I'll never forget my first trip to Charleston," designer Mary Douglas Drysdale says. "It's been one of my favorite cities ever since. Charleston has always represented the best in style and elegant detail." For the master bedroom, the Washington, D.C., designer sought to speak to the past while looking to the future of Southern style. "I thought that a deeply colored room with hints of green would be unexpected yet very comfortable," she says. To set a cozy, restful mood, she coated walls in Benjamin Moore's earthy "Ashwood Moss." To juxtapose the moody walls, Drysdale called on plenty of airy whites. White paint covers a new mantel that she designed to take the place of an original fireplace that had been removed. A custom bed from Theodore Alexander with a soaring headboard tufted in Kravet fabric injects an additional light, bright note, as does a dreamy cloud chandelier. A Stark carpet, alpaca throws, and handmade linen sheets layer in tactile elements and a feeling of artisanship, something very Charlestonian, Drysdale says.

Master Bath Suite Ili Hidalgo-Nilsson of Terracotta Design Build Co. in Decatur, Georgia, made the master bath the ultimate retreat, incorporating indulgent bathing and showering experiences—and a handy beverage station. A DXV soaking tub sits in a paneled niche that feels like a secret sanctuary. The shower, meanwhile, features a sophisticated combination of surfaces from Crossville: "Snow Flower" tile from the Yin + Yang collection on the ceiling and in mosaic tile on the floor, "State of Grace" porcelain slabs on the walls and bench. Shower fixtures are from DXV. The vanity area features handsome stained-wood cabinetry with a pair of undermount sinks and widespread faucets set in "Film Noir" unpolished porcelain from Crossville. "Envisioned" wallcovering from Kravet placed behind twin mirrors gives the look of marble. Sconces interject the warm glow of brass. A beverage station—built into rich wood cabinetry that matches the vanity—boasts a Thermador coffee machine and refrigerator drawer. The setup eliminates the need to trot down three flights of stairs to get morning coffee. "The luxury of those little details is important," Hidalgo-Nilsson says.

MASTER BATH SUITE
ILI HIDALGO-NILSSON

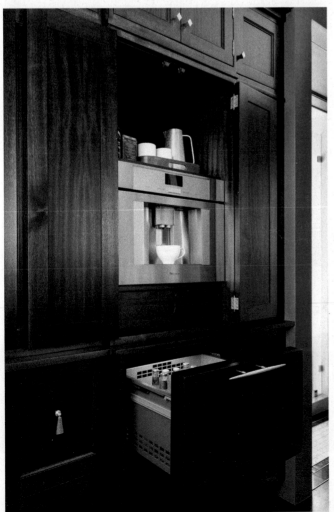

LADIES' DRAWING ROOM
MALLORY MATHISON GLENN

Ladies' Drawing Room Atlanta designer Mallory Mathison Glenn envisioned this room as a retreat for repose, reading, and revelry—dignified revelry, of course. To create the perfect envelope, she called on Benjamin Moore's "Claret." "It's a pleasing coral that gives a warm glow to the pretty faces of ladies playing cards, taking afternoon tea, or penning correspondence," Glenn says. For a collected feel, she incorporated a variety of contemporary artworks along with French and English antiques, chinoiserie, and blanc de Chine. Old pieces comfortably commingle with new Wesley Hall club chairs dressed in a lively animal print and a desk chair clad in blue leather. "Coral, celadon, aqua, and peacock with punches of citron create a layered, elegant palette," Glenn says. "The tone is vibrancy partnered with delicacy."

Mezzanine & Front Porch (page 71) Easy evenings sipping sweet tea in the cool air are made even more enjoyable—and stylish—by Charlotte Lucas, who shaped porches that are the envy of the neighborhood. Painted floors enlivened with checkerboard or Greek-key patterns set the stage for inviting seating areas. "I didn't want to simply line the porch with rockers," the Charlotte designer says. "There needed to be seating versatile to any occasion." To that end, she created a dining nook anchored by a comfy Woodard love seat on the front porch. On the mezzanine, cane-back Woodard rockers outfit a conversation spot, and a curtained hideaway features a porch swing from Ballard Designs. Schumacher's "Yangtze River" fabric lends a satisfying pop of contemporary color in a traditional package while lanterns from Bevolo Gas & Electric Lights on the front porch mesh with classic columns.

CARRIAGE HOUSE
GUEST SUITE
OLIVIA BROCK

Carriage House Guest Suite Call it serendipity: As Olivia Brock brainstormed the design for the carriage house guest suite, a copy of *The Gardens of Bunny Mellon* just happened to arrive at her office. "I couldn't help but be inspired by Mrs. Mellon's gardens, as well as the interiors of her home," says the preservation-minded creative who founded Torrance Mitchell Designs. "I wanted this room to be beautiful but feel lived in." First, she assessed the existing architecture of the space, which included exposed rafters, painted brick, and new drywall. "I not only wanted to unify the space but also to call attention to the history of the building as a former kitchen house by giving it a no-frills feeling," the Charleston designer says. She had paint stripped off the beams to expose the original wood finish and covered the drywall with traditional beaded board. Painting window trim green draws the eye outside, where garden views tantalize over neatly trimmed café curtains. A low-profile bed from Ballard Designs, upholstered in Lee Jofa fabric, comfortably snuggles into the low-ceilinged room. The adjoining bath is both clean-lined and luxurious, featuring an expanse of Crossville tile, a console sink from DXV, and a sumptuous array of brass fixtures and hardware.

LEOPARD'S DEN
ANGIE HRANOWSKY

Leopard's Den Cozy was the goal for this dormer bedroom designed by Angie Hranowsky—cozy with sexy sass, that is. For softness, the Charleston designer enveloped the room in upholstery. "Using a single fabric disguises the angles and pitches created by the gable roof and makes the room more intimate," Hranowsky says. Because the Rose Cumming fabric is pink leopard print, it also "turns up the volume a bit," Hranowsky says. She called on a mix of prints and colorways for upholstery, drapery, and pillow fabrics to achieve a collected look. It suits her mélange of furniture pieces, all antique and vintage finds that she refreshed with new fabric. Benjamin Moore's "Black Raspberry" paint on the window frame, bookcase, trim, and doors connects to the hues of a chair cushion and a Christopher Spitzmiller lamp. "I chose the purple paint color for its unexpectedness and to keep with the warm pink and red tones," Hranowsky says. "The deep purple, garnet red, and rich greens also make the palette feel adult—I didn't want the room, with its primarily pink fabric, to feel like a little girl's space." An abaca rug adds texture to the room without competing with the patterned fabrics.

Artist's Studio & Bath Cameron Schwabenton of Cameron Stewart design in Charleston saw this tucked-away spot on the third floor as the perfect artist's nest. "This little space called out to be inspiring, colorful, and clever yet visually serene enough for ideas to flow," she says. While envisioning the design, Schwabenton stepped into the mind of her grandmother, an artist who worked for Walt Disney. "Some of the colors were inspired by her favorite shades of blush," Schwabenton says. She bathed walls and ceiling in Benjamin Moore's "Orleans Violet." "Depending on the time of day, the color shifts from pink to lavender," she says. Deep blue-green on velvet draperies anchors the room and draws the eye up. Civil War-era epaulets used as tiebacks act as historical art while their cascades make exquisite trim. Ivory-hue midcentury chairs introduce a sculptural, modern shape perched on classic legs with brass mounts. Greek-key trim on the ottoman skirt nods to the home's Greek Revival architecture. In the bath, black and white make a simple graphic statement. A sink skirt layers in softness; brass accents supply a touch of glitz. To make the most of limited real estate, Schwabenton continued the vanity mirror up the angled wall above the sink. It cheerfully reflects light throughout the tiny room. 🏠

For more information, see sources on page 118

Kitchen 2.0

CRAFTING EXTRAORDINARY KITCHENS IS NOTHING NEW FOR MICK DE GIULIO. **BUT THIS SPACE IS.**

WRITTEN BY SALLY FINDER WEEPIE
PHOTOGRAPHY BY WERNER STRAUBE
PRODUCED BY HILARY ROSE

MELDING GENRES AND MELTING BOUNDARIES,
DE GIULIO WORKED WITH DESIGN-SAVVY
HOMEOWNER YOANNA KULAS TO SHAPE
SOMETHING MORE THAN A COOKING SPACE.
HERE'S HIS FORMULA FOR TODAY'S
NEW KITCHEN-CENTRIC HOME.

Gathering area A backdrop of Benjamin Moore's "Decorator's White" unites the living area with the kitchen. Generous windows are outlined in black, framing outdoor views.
Preceding pages Luxurious simplicity reigns in a space outfitted with Carrara marble, Sub-Zero refrigerators, and furniture that homeowner Yoanna Kulas specified from Belgian atelier AM Designs.

WE'RE CONTINUING AN EVOLUTION THAT MAKES SPACES MORE LIVABLE."
—designer Mick De Giulio

1. ERASE ARTIFICIAL BARRIERS

"There's no question that an open living plan is now my clients' favorite idea," Mick De Giulio says. "With the Kulases' Chicago house, we're continuing an evolution that makes spaces more livable." Nothing interrupts the flow of activity. Life unfolds organically, and the kitchen is fully empowered to live up to its oft-touted billing as heart of the home.

The open plan also acknowledges our intrinsic need for natural light. "People have to have light flowing through a space in order to feel alive," De Giulio says.

He took care, though, to carve out intimate areas within the larger space. The cooking zone, the island, the dining table, the soft sofas by the fireplace—each spot is right-sized, cozy, and utterly comfortable.

2. TAKE A CUE FROM MARIE KONDO

If the popularity of the Japanese downsizing and organizing queen is any indication, we're all ready to do with a little less stuff and a lot less drama. So De Giulio focused on essential beauty rather than unnecessary ornamentation. "Yoanna and I left only things important to the way they really live," he says.

A soothing, seamless space with no pretensions makes it easy to escape the artifices and overload of the modern world. Architectural and design elements serve as sculpture, art in a home that puts no priority on tchotchke.

3. REMEMBER WHAT'S IRRESISTIBLE ABOUT WHITE KITCHENS

White is classic—it will never go out of style. White is calm, fresh, and clean. And like a white plate, a white kitchen makes whatever it holds look amazing.

Here, the tantalizing bits of eye candy include a reclaimed-pine farm table modified to house a cooktop, a pine table and bench, stainless-steel refrigerators and an oven console, and plenty of Carrara marble. "The wood grain, metal, and stone become visually tactile against the white backdrop," De Giulio says.

4. BE HONEST

"For this home, I liked the idea of something very simple and humble," De Giulio says. "There are no exotic veneers, metals, or stone." Authenticity and artisanship make their own statement.

Plank board walls recall the familiar shiplap of farmhouse style. Exposed ceiling beams and white oak cabinetry wear a whitewash finish that allows the grain to peek through. "There are crosscut saw marks on every door—elements of texture," De Giulio says.

"The cabinetry isn't a focal point—it's a backdrop," he says. "It was fun to think in a different way with the cabinets and counters not the focus of attention."

Countertops are a simple type of honed marble. Humble hot-rolled steel frames shelves and forms the insert for the ventilation hood. The refrigerators stand uncloaked by cabinetry panels. "They look like two honest refrigerators," De Giulio says. "Things here are what they are."

5. ACE THE GEOMETRY TEST

"This design is different in that it's non-aligned—not axial like many of my designs," De Giulio says. "That makes it feel more layered and more informal."

The island cozies up near the fridge, but it's not rigidly plumb-lined with the edge of the cooling wall. Nor does it unnecessarily sprawl to match up with the cooktop table. Nothing is forced; everything feels comfortable.

"Proportions are really well-considered," De Giulio says. "In fact, proportion is my favorite thing about this kitchen."

Attention is paid to details as small as the fine line between each wall plank—"it gives a horizontal feeling that's calming," the designer says. And that proves his axiom: A great kitchen has a magic that transforms the physical room into a feeling.

Cooktop Built into a pine console, the Wolf rangetop is fed by a gas line ingeniously hidden in a hefty table leg. **Designer** Mick De Giulio. **Sink** While it's surrounded by Carrara marble, the sink is actually tough stainless steel. Teak cutting boards slide where they're needed. **Ovens** A Wolf oven, convection oven, and warming drawer share space in a freestanding console. De Giulio gave its stainless-steel sides a shiplap look.

6. LET A HOME CHEF CHANNEL HER INNER GIADA DE LAURENTIIS

"The Kulases—and so many of my clients—cook every day and like sitting down as a family for meals," De Giulio says. "High-function appliances are really important."

He reshaped the ubiquitous work triangle into efficient stations that easily accommodate multiple chefs and their helpers. "It's a big space that operates like a small space," De Giulio says.

A freestanding rangetop is set into a pine table that offers plenty of prep space—and marble cutting boards that fit neatly over the wood surface. Alongside, another console, this one metal, holds an arsenal of ovens. A quick pivot away, the primary sink pairs with an expanse of marble counters suitable for tossing a salad or rolling dough. Within the orbit of both the cooking zone and the island, twin refrigerators hold a bounty of fresh produce and an array of beverages.

Nothing is hidden or hard to find. Glass fronts on the refrigerators make it easy to spot what you need. So do open storage shelves, arranged so guests are comfortable setting a place for dinner or cleaning up afterward. Even the ventilation hood is situated with open sight lines in mind.

7. TEACH A TWO-STORY HOME TO LIVE LIKE A RANCH

This is a multilevel home, but everything the empty nesters need for everyday life is on the main level—including the master suite. Guests have privacy on the upper level while Yoanna and her husband enjoy no-stairs living.

Following the model set in the kitchen, the master suite is a serene, flowing space that celebrates honest materials and abundant light. "How it's set up makes it successful," De Giulio says.

The sleeping area organically flows into a sitting area. Beyond it, a sink peninsula offers subtle delineation between the sleeping space and shower. A freestanding tub feels like a piece of sculpture. And because the room is at the rear of the house, opening to a fenced back courtyard, there

Stairway The staircase needs no ornamentation. Its shape injects a sculptural moment into the home's interior architecture.

Closet Painted plank cabinetry opens to reveal storage for shoes and clothing.

are no worries about prying eyes. Bubble baths can be savored under the stars. A stone wall, meanwhile, acts as both art form and privacy screen for the shower, home to an airy floating shelf and a convenient shampoo niche.

Behind the shower, multiple closets efficiently organize fashion-forward Yoanna's clothes, shoes, and accessories. Color coordinating is easy: Sunshine floods in from skylights to supplement interior lights that turn on automatically when a closet door opens.

"You can see why I personally would love to live here," De Giulio says. "I love how this house functions. I love how it feels. Truly, it's one of the most livable houses I've ever worked on." 🔲

Designer: Mick De Giulio   **Architect:** Michael Abraham
Interior design: Yoanna Kulas

For more information, see sources on page 118

Shower Carrara marble unfurls across the walls, floor, and ceiling of the shower, outfitted with a Dornbracht mixer.

Powder room Honed marble and wood paneling reappear in the guest bath.

Bedroom Expansive windows let light (and pups) rush in from the patio, screened for privacy.
Bath The sleeping area connects to the bath space, where a Lacava tub injects shapely curves. The white-painted wood vanity provides storage on both sides. Like the cabinets, the suspended mirror exudes farmhouse charm.

Light at Heart

DESIGNER
RAY BOOTH
REFRESHES AN
ANGLOPHILIC
BALTIMORE
HOME FOR AN
ALL-AMERICAN
FAMILY

WRITTEN BY JENNY BRADLEY PFEFFER
PHOTOGRAPHY BY HELEN NORMAN
PRODUCED BY ELEANOR ROPER

Cnglish in its inception but heartily American in its outcome, Blake and Angie Cordish's Maryland home is both refined and gregarious—the Audrey Hepburn of Baltimore estates.

Built in the early 1900s, the Colonial Revival house sits amid rolling hills in a bucolic setting that brings to mind the stately homes of England's lush countryside. To restore what was perfect about the house while giving it an updated spin, Blake and Angie turned to acclaimed architectural and design firm McAlpine, their partner in work on previous residences.

"Angie and Blake were inspired by the great hotels of London," designer Ray Booth says. "The concept was of this being an English country house in influence yet more relaxed in its posture."

The extraordinary setting was a guiding force. From the front door, one's eyes are drawn immediately through the entry to French doors that frame the pastoral setting beyond. In fact, the commodious entry may have been a little too open. "It almost gave away too much too quickly," Booth says. "We added two-story sheers to frame the opening. It's like a punctuation mark on a sentence. It slows you down—gives you a moment to stop, appreciate, and then move on."

Conservatory A gateleg table and sundry seating options form a carefree furniture arrangement, intentionally unaligned with the architecture of the room. The slipcovered "Paige" sofa is by Kerry Joyce for Dessin Fournir.
Entry A tufted sofa from Ferrell Mittman anchors a sitting area in the sizable space. **Preceding pages** Angie Cordish strolls with her daughter. Cascading sheers were installed in the entry for visual impact. The whimsical wing chair is from Madeline Stuart.

There is much to appreciate here. Original architectural details were restored, providing a stage for an array of cultivated furniture pieces. A center table with a weighty, animated base and a stone top becomes a vivacious partner for a curvy wing chair and a tufted sofa. Scroll-back chairs and ottomans with dressmaker skirts offer perchable moments in a house that embraces entertaining.

Playing off the entry's genteel palette, Booth used dollops of caramel and plum in the living room, creating a light-filled space that is welcoming with a dash of formality. A streamlined sofa in cream-color linen pairs beautifully with architectural details that quietly let the furnishings shine yet are extroverted enough to avoid wallflower status. A slipper chair upholstered in a patterned velvet and an armchair with playful lines gambol with a tufted ottoman that invites guests to kick up their feet. "We chose furniture that was comfortable and referred back to something a bit more English," Booth says. "Rolled arms, tufting, pieces that were more traditional in form yet weren't wildly refined."

The antithesis of the light, bright living room and entry, the dining room wears a moody caramel-infused palette, an intentional choice to encourage close conversation in candlelight. Separated into two distinct seating areas, the large space reconceives the traditional dining format—reinterpreting it for a family that entertains often.

On one side, an intimate setting lined with bookshelves offers a casual, club-like approach to dining—ideal for small groups and cocktail gatherings. Cozied up to a marble fireplace, a low table is surrounded by myriad seating options including a tufted mohair-clad

chair and a coquettish skirted settee. A silk portiere and a smoky glass chandelier with crystal notes inject romance and femininity.

A more traditional dining table flanked by scroll-back chairs and a slipcovered banquette acts as host to large dinner parties and holiday get-togethers. Streamlined, the corner is sans chandelier—a thoughtful choice to eliminate unnecessary overhead distractions. Instead, Booth had wiring installed through the table legs to illuminate low-slung shaded votives. The result is an experience that hints at low-lit, whispered dinners at an exclusive club.

In the kitchen, classic elements meld with an industrial aesthetic to shape a setting where the culinary can also be the theatrical. Elegant touches such as a black-and-white checkerboard floor, a solid marble backsplash, and an Irish wake table balance a plenitude of stainless steel.

The command center of the house, the space is as family-centric as it is dramatic. A faux-leather-clad banquette defies spills. Handsome armchairs are slipcovered in outdoor fabric for practicality. A working pantry nestled behind the range means messes—and sippy cups—can be easily hidden from view. Polished and practical, it's the design gold standard.

Living room A mix of styles and fabrics—velvet on the Soane slipper chair and linen on the Lucca & Co. sofa—provides a gathered-over-time aesthetic.
Dining room Separate areas—one intimate, the other for large gatherings—let the dining room multitask. A portiere adds romance. The slipcovered banquette was designed to be roomy and muted—allowing the large custom table to be more conspicuous. "You need some things to be backup singers," designer Ray Booth says. "Not everything can sing at the top of its voice."

Kitchen Family-friendly meets Old Hollywood. Slipcovered chairs and a faux-leather tufted sofa gather around an Irish wake table. Industrial-inspired elements, such as the stainless-steel appliances and custom hood with polished-nickel detailing, play up the black-and-white checkerboard floor.

Equally pitch-perfect, the conservatory echoes the kitchen's sharply contrasted palette—beginning with a black-and-white mosaic tile floor. Structured and playful, a lacquered ceiling with an alternating diagonal pattern reflects the greenery outdoors, surreptitiously bringing the outdoors in. Dark lacquered mullions and muntins visually fall away, letting the rolling landscape draw the eye in a room intended to highlight outdoors rather than in.

"We like to paint windows dark," Booth says. "Our eyes are attracted to light, so using light colors can cage you in. We naturally look past a dark color to the light colors beyond."

Yin to the conservatory's yang, the luminous master bedroom is enfolded in a pale palette of creamy white and lavender. A bookcase with fluted detail adds gravity and texture to a low-slung upholstered headboard. Two chaises pulled toe-to-toe become a graceful makeshift window seat punctuated with gingham pillows. A shapely glass-drop chandelier injects a contemporary yet still feminine note.

"We couldn't play by all the rules," Booth says. "This is a period home, but a modern family lives here. It needs life and exuberance."

Interior designer: Ray Booth

For more information, see sources on page 118

Master bedroom Serenity reigns in a space highlighted by a pair of shapely daybeds and a sparkling chandelier, both from Ochre. **Master bath** Known for using drapery as an emotional device, Booth wraps the master bath in luxurious texture. The custom multitier chandelier by Jaeger features silver-leaf agate panels by Ironies. **Exterior** Poised and postured, the architecture of the early 1900s home was honored. **Family** Angie and her son enjoy time on the home's well-manicured grounds.

ONE OF THE JOYOUS THINGS ABOUT THIS HOUSE IS ITS BEAUTIFUL LIGHT." —designer Ray Booth

Porch and lawn Engaging the lush setting was of the utmost importance in the home's design. A classic palette, a charming porch swing, and a sofa and chairs from Michael Taylor Designs let the landscape do the heavy lifting. Draperies offer an air of romance. "Plantation" chairs by Uwharrie are at the ready for relaxation. 🏛

BEST OF BOTH

DESIGNER AMY MEIER JOINS PAST AND PRESENT, CLEAN-LINED AND CLASSIC IN A NEW CALIFORNIA HOME

WRITTEN AND PRODUCED BY JENNY BRADLEY PFEFFER
PHOTOGRAPHY BY SHADE DEGGES

From any perspective, David and Sonja Brockett's La Jolla, California, home defies classification. Though newly built, it feels as if it's been firmly planted on this magical plot of land for decades. Slyly beach bungalow in style, it flaunts details more often found in New England Colonials. Yet its formal tendencies are balanced with clearcut casual moments. This is a home unerringly straightforward in its contradictions.

The cornerstone attitude of this home is innately old and new, beachy and traditional. The property on which it sits had long been home to La Jolla's original (now relocated) train station—a storied structure from which David had run his family dental practice for 30 years. Hoping to convert the commercial space into their home upon retirement, the Brocketts discovered that, sadly, the building was no longer structurally sound.

Undeterred, they brought in designer Amy Meier and architect Endre Bartanyi to imagine a historically minded home that recalls the structure it replaced while starting its own unique story.

"The beach bungalow was really our jumping-off point because Hawaii is a very meaningful place for David and Sonja," Meier says. "But they also craved a sense of history and the visual intrigue that one sees in Colonial and Federal-era homes."

Dining room The blue of ocean waves makes a subtle splash in the neutral dining room. Vintage Italian chairs are upholstered in Kravet fabric. An Urban Electric pendant echoes the shape of the custom table.
Entry Pieces personal to the family, such as these antique sugar bins, make the home meaningful. **Exterior** The new home charmingly melds beach bungalow and traditional styles. **Preceding pages** The living room shows designer Amy Meier's mastery of the mix. An antique fireplace surround, sconces, and a pendant mingle beautifully with "Rising Moon" chairs from Rose Tarlow and a custom coffee table formed of Silestone.

Kitchen The classic white kitchen gets a stunning twist from a watery-hue backsplash, stained-wood island, and one-of-a-kind bar stools. Waterworks fixtures and pendants contribute to a sophisticated amalgam of metals.

The balancing act begins with a floor plan that welcomingly throws its arms wide open as it also illuminates refined moments, such as custom millwork and gracious antiques. In the entry, unexpected elements with sentimental weight instill a sense of place and create a home that feels lived in and time honed. Against gray-white walls, antique sugar bins hold court under a photograph of the Brocketts' Hawaii vacation home, which happens to be just down the road from a sugar mill. The bins are so cherished that the space was designed with their dimensions in mind.

"The sugar bins were just perfect, a manifestation of everything we wanted to create in the home," Meier says.

Simultaneously formal and carefree, the living room boasts the same confident coastal palette as the entry. Slightly enigmatic, it evokes misty mornings and the merging of sand and sea. Reclaimed-wood floors, millwork wall panels, and a salvaged 19th-century cheminée add patina and depth. The curves of a baby grand piano and two sleekly sculptural armchairs pair with a strictly clean-lined coffee table, organic plaster sconces, and unornamented linen draperies. It's a sublimely cohesive room rich with contrasts.

The visual give-and-take continues to play out in the dining room, where antique chairs upholstered with a graphic fabric surround a more contemporary pedestal table. Textural hand-troweled plaster with a metallic tinge complements classic wainscoting. A white-painted cabinet interjects a fresh twist.

"We wanted a traditional feature that announces 'This is the dining room,' but we didn't want it to be so formal that it seemed out of

Master bedroom The wood tones of a new bed from Bolier mesh with an antique French bench. Kravet drapery fabric furthers the geometric spin of contemporary art. **Family** David Brockett enjoys time with his grandson.

SOMETIMES IT'S SIMPLY ABOUT LETTING PIECES SPEAK FOR THEMSELVES."
—designer Amy Meier

place," Meier says. The solution was to build a custom cabinet in front of a wall of exterior windows—ensuring a lighthearted, airy version of the traditional built-in. Pottery in sand- and sea-inspired hues fills the ethereal shelves.

The mist, sea, and sand palette meanders into a kitchen that feels both contemporary and deeply rooted. A hand-painted tile backsplash in shades of blue and green shimmers against light cabinets and quartz countertops the color of shoreline fog. Striking bar stools upholstered with luscious mahogany-hue leather inject a sense of weightiness, balancing the light scheme. A contemporary sculpture punctuates the space with dramatic effect.

Similarly theatrical, a black-on-black painting by James Austin Murray elegantly juxtaposes off-white walls, reclaimed beams, and a mahogany four-poster in the master bedroom. Fabrics with subtle pattern and organic movement soften hard lines.

"I feel like the bedroom was a synergistic combination of everyone's desires," Meier says. "Sonja loves black and white, David wanted an interesting ceiling, and I wanted it to be cozy and inviting. The result is a kind of retreat. It feels warm, yet there is high contrast in materials and color."

A serene extension of the bedroom, the master bath epitomizes a focus on quality versus quantity. A French drapier table topped with stone forms a vanity. Floor planks in a boxed mitered layout accentuate a pewter tub. Cognac-hue draperies meld with wood tones.

"Sometimes it's simply about letting pieces speak for themselves," Meier says. "If the pieces we choose are the right pieces, we don't need to dress them up or shout them down. We just let them speak." ⊞

Interior designer: Amy Meier **Architect:** Endre Bartanyi

For more information, see sources on page 118

Master bath A freestanding Waterworks tub takes center stage in an elegant bath rich with architectural detail.

Reader's Resource

For more information about the stories shown in this issue, contact the professionals and sources listed here. Contact information has been verified, but we cannot guarantee the availability of items or services. No information is available about items not listed.

PAGES 57–60
KITCHENS: FRENCH CONNECTION

Architect: Christy Blumenfeld, Blume Architecture, Dallas; 972/743-2835; christy@blumearchitecture.com; blumearchitecture.com.
Interior designer: Heidi Arwine, Heidi Arwine Interiors, Coppell, Texas; 214/505-9189; info@heidiarwineinteriors.com; heidiarwineinteriors.com.
MAIN KITCHEN—**Lower cabinetry, range** "Château": La Cornue; lacornueusa.com.
Ceiling-mounted shelving custom design: Heidi Arwine, Heidi Arwine Interiors, heidiarwineinteriors.com; Christy Blumenfeld, blumearchitecture.com. **Fabrication of shelving and vent hood** custom: Seal Tex; sealtex.com.
Countertops, backsplash, table top "Danby" marble: contact local cut-stone suppliers. **Faucet** "Traditional Pulldown" in Matte Black: Waterstone; waterstoneco.com. **Sink:** Rohl; rohlhome.com. **Ceiling beams:** Faux Wood Beams; fauxwoodbeams.com.
Pop-up outlets on countertops: S-Box; the-sbox.com. **Pendant lights at table** Visual Comfort through Circa Lighting; circalighting.com. **Table base** antique lathe: Uncommon Market; uncommonmarketdallas.com.
Bar stools "Loom" in Platinum Rope and Light Gray fabric: Orient Express; orientexpressfurniture.com.
Windows: Kolbe; kolbewindows.com.
BAKING KITCHEN—**Refrigerator, freezer, steam oven** integrated with cabinets: Sub-Zero; subzero-wolf.com.
Refrigerator hardware: Roseland Icebox; iceboxes.com. **Countertops, backsplash, table top** honed "Via Lactea" granite: contact local cut-stone suppliers.
Backsplash tile: Walker Zanger; walkerzanger.com.

PAGES 70–87
CHARLESTON IN CHARGE
SOUTHERN STYLE NOW DESIGNER SHOWHOUSE CHARLESTON, SOUTH CAROLINA
PAGE 70. GARDEN—**Landscape architect:** Glen Gardner; 843/722-5885; gardnerla.com.
Exterior lighting and candleholder "Governor Flush-Mount Lantern" and "Pool House Lantern" in Aged Copper: Bevolo Gas & Electric Lights; bevolo.com. **White Leinfelder iron table:** antique. **Clear chairs** "LeisureMod Murray Lucite Stackable Molded Dining Side Chair": Houzz; houzz.com. **White cast-iron table, large planters, lead elephant sculpture, pots** antique and vintage: Charleston Garden Works; charlestongardenworks.com.
PAGE 71. FRONT PORCH—**Interior designer:** Charlotte Lucas, 416 Providence Road, Suite 3, Charlotte, NC 28207; 980/859-7499; charlottelucasdesign.com. **Paint on shutters** "Polo Blue" 2062-10, **floor base coat** Super Spek industrial enamel, **Greek key border** "Mopboard Black": Benjamin Moore; benjaminmoore.com. **White table and chairs:** vintage. **Love seat behind table** "Cane Love Seat": Woodard Furniture; woodard-furniture.com. **Love-seat fabric** "Yangtze River" in Jade: Schumacher; fschumacher.com. **Pink pillow** custom in "Markham–Candy AM100108-717": Kravet; kravet.com. **Planter** "Evelyn Terra Cotta Bust Planter": Ballard Designs; ballarddesigns.com. **Chairs with caned backs:** vintage. **Chair-seat fabric** "Yangtze River" in Jade: Schumacher; fschumacher.com. **Pink rug runner:** Nashville Rug Gallery; nashvilleruggallery.com.
PAGE 72. CARRIAGE HOUSE DEN—**Interior designer:** Traci Zeller, 2935 Providence Road, Suite 202, Charlotte, NC 28211; 980/272-0234; tracizeller.com. **Ceiling paint** "Strawberry Yogurt," **wall and trim paint** "Cloud White": Benjamin Moore;

benjaminmoore.com. **Drapery hardware:** Helser Brothers; helserbrothers.com.
Draperies custom, **fabric:** available through Traci Zeller Interiors; tracizeller.com. **Sofa at left** "Jennifer" in Gabrielle Blush: CR Laine; crlaine.com. **Center pillow on sofa:** designer's collection, made from Hermès scarf. **Brown pillow** "Martin" in Café: CR Laine; crlaine.com. **Print pillow on sofa** "Arrowheads" in Camellia/Berry: Block & Brayer; blockandbrayer.com. **Fringe** "Oyster": CR Laine; crlaine.com. **Lamp with green shade** "Brushstroke" in brown: Bunny Williams Home; bunnywilliamshome.com.
Lampshade Lacquered in Benjamin Moore #630 Martha's Vineyard: Newport Lamp & Shade; newportlampandshade.com.
Stacking tables "Savoye Shagreen Nest of Tables": Woodbridge Furniture; woodbridgefurniture.com. **Jug under stacking tables** "Mayme Vase": Ballard Designs; ballarddesigns.com. **Ottoman** "Columbus" in "Martin" fuchsia fabric with "Wood" band, **green daybed** "Liv" #2040 in "Kate Ivy" fabric: CR Laine; crlaine.com.
Pillows on daybed custom in "Mountain Laurel" fabric: blockandbrayer.com. **Trim** "Wooly Sable" fringe: CR Laine; crlaine.com. **Blanket** "Avalon" throw: Hermès; hermes.com. **Octagonal table** "Savoye Shagreen Spot Table": Woodbridge Furniture; woodbridgefurniture.com. **Floor lamp** "Sommerard Triple-Arm Floor Lamp" by Aerin: Circa Lighting; circalighting.com.
Chairs "Francois" in "Polar Bear Snow" fabric, **pillows on chairs** custom in "Gabrielle Blush" fabric with "Pumice–Mini Pleat" band: CR Laine; crlaine.com. **Throws on chairs** "Classic Herringbone" in Dune: Ballard Designs; ballarddesigns.com.
Artwork over chairs *Mixed Media Abstract* by William McClure: Anne Neilson Fine Art; anneneilsonfineart.com. **Carpet** "Antilocarpa" in Almond: Stark Carpet; starkcarpet.com.
PAGE 72. PARLOR—**Interior designer:** Matthew Carter, 115 Clay Ave., Lexington, KY 40502; 859/266-4485; matthewcarterinteriors.com. **Ceiling paint** "Old Country" OC-76, **trim paint** "Capitol White," **wall paint** "Chartreuse 2024-10": Benjamin Moore; benjaminmoore.com. **Draperies** custom in "Tucker": Sister Parish; sisterparishdesign.com. **Drapery hardware:** custom. **Bamboo shelves, gold mirror, candles, statue of seated man, plant basket, carved chest, black metal art over painting with stand, painting, ram's-head lamp, ivory table, stool, gold bench, square coffee table, orange and purple painting** by Santoyo, **painting of horses and riders** by Claude Grosperrin: vintage. **Blue lamp** "Haan" in Robin's Egg: Christopher Spitzmiller; christopherspitzmiller.com. **Floral chair**

with wooden legs vintage, **fabric** "Jardin Des Plantes Prints" in Multi; Quadrille Fabrics; quadrillefabrics.com. **Striped chair** "Small Slipper Chair": Billy Baldwin Studio; billybaldwinstudio.com. **Chair fabric** "Inverness" in light red: Carleton V Ltd.; carletonvltd.com. **Brown sofa** "Style 9150 Cameron" in brown linen velvet: O'Henry House; ohenryhouseltd.com. **Carpet** "Kamali" in Wheat: Stark Carpet; starkcarpet.com.

PAGE 73. Interior designer: Lindsey Coral Harper, 247 E. 60th St., 2nd Floor, New York, NY 10022; 212/686-3610; lchinteriors.com.
ENTRY & STAIR TOWER — **Wallcovering** custom, "Peony" with background PC-25 and details in silver: Gracie Studio; graciestudio.com. **Trim paint** "Slate CW-700": Benjamin Moore; benjamin moore.com. **Ceiling light** "Warwick Medium Lantern" by E.F. Chapman in brass: Circa Lighting; circalighting.com. **Carpet on stairway** "Kubra 2" in Charcoal: Stark Carpet; starkcarpet.com. **Rugs:** vintage: Fine Rugs of Charleston; finerugsofcharleston.com. **Black chairs with gold detailing:** vintage: Fritz Porter; fritzporter.com. **Queen Anne console table:** Parc Monceau Antiques Ltd; parcmonceauatl.com. **Magazine holder under table:** vintage: available at Lindsey Coral Harper Interiors; lchinteriors.com. **Pink-and-gold bird:** designer's own. **Curtain fabric** "Colette" in Charcoal: Schumacher; fschumacher.com. **Curtain lining** #32653 in Papaya: Duralee; duralee.com. **Fringe trim** "Celine Ombre" brush fringe in 03 Slate: Samuel & Sons; samuelandsons.com. **Mirror** antique: John Rosselli Antiques; johnrosselliantiques.com. **Lamp** "Single Wide Zig Zag" in Platinum Luster: Christopher Spitzmiller; christopherspitzmiller.com. **Lampshade** neutral wicker light linen: John Rosselli Antiques; johnrosselliantiques.com. **Picture lights** "Frame Maker" by E.F. Chapman in brass: Circa Lighting; circalighting.com. **Artwork at left in white frame** Pitcher with Circles by Vicki Sher: The George Gallery; georgegalleryart.com.

PAGES 75–76. DINING ROOM — **Interior designer:** MA Allen; 1020 Glenwood Ave., Raleigh, NC 27605; 919/834-8333; maalleninteriors.com. **Ceiling paint** "Capitol White," **trim paints** "Capitol White" and "Capitol Black": Benjamin Moore; benjaminmoore.com. **Chandelier** "Halcyon Large Three-Tier" by Kelly Wearstler: Circa Lighting; circalighting.com. **Wallcovering** "New World" hand-painted in sepia tones: Gracie Studio; graciestudio.com. **Painting** A Gathering of Monarchs mixed media and neon by Louis St. Lewis and Nate Sheaffer: Allison Sprock Fine Art; allisonsprockfineart.net. **Chest** "Lancer Chest of Drawers" in Renaissance and Ebony finish: Chaddock; chaddockhome.com. **Silver champagne cooler, ice bucket, cocktail shaker, tray, green cordial glasses, pink compote glasses, pink goblets, silver water goblets:** Replacements, Ltd.; replacements.com. **Dining table** "Pauline Dining Table" in Renaissance finish: Chaddock; chaddockhome.com. **Dining**

chairs "Vintage Maison Jansen Side Chairs": MA Allen Interiors; maalleninteriors.com. **Dining armchairs** "Chastaing" in Weathered Cream finish with accents in Ebony: Chaddock; chaddockhome.com. DETAIL — **Chandelier** "Halcyon Large Three-Tier" by Kelly Wearstler: Circa Lighting; circalighting.com. **Wallcovering** "New World" hand-painted in sepia tones: Gracie Studio; graciestudio.com. **Painting over mantel:** Mallory Page; mallorypage.com. **Chairs flanking fireplace** "Georgia Hall Chair": Chaddock; chaddockhome.com. **Pink compote glasses, pink goblets, silver water goblets:** Replacements, Ltd.; replacements.com. **Napkins** custom: MA Allen Interiors; maalleninteriors.com. **Dining table** "Pauline" in Renaissance finish: Chaddock; chaddockhome.com. **Dining chairs** "Vintage Maison Jansen Side Chairs": MA Allen Interiors; maalleninteriors.com. **Dining armchairs** "Chastaing" in Weathered Cream finish with accents in Ebony: Chaddock; chaddockhome.com.

PAGES 76–78. KITCHEN — **Interior designers:** Michael Mitchell and Tyler Hill, 438 King St., Charleston, SC 29403; 843/564-0034; mitchellhillinc.com. **Ceiling** custom design by Tyler Hill in steel-and-mesh screen finished in brushed steel, aged brass, and mirrored panels: Mitchell Hill; mitchellhillinc.com. **Wall, trim, and cabinet paint** "Tavern Gray": Benjamin Moore; benjaminmoore.com. **Cabinets:** Tupper Builders Inc.; 843/864-3615. **Cabinet pulls** "Newport Knob" and "Westwood Pull" in satin brass: Emtek; emtek.com. **Range hood** custom design by Michael Mitchell in tinted mirror and brushed steel, manufactured by Avrett with glass supplied by Glass Act Productions: Mitchell Hill; mitchellhillinc.com. **Tile backsplash** Yin + Yang collection in "Moon Gate": Crossville; crossvilleinc.com. **Pot filler** "Traditional Pot Filler" in polished chrome: DXV; dxv.com. **Range** "Pro Harmony" 36-inch 6-burner: Thermador; thermador. com. **Countertop** black soapstone: Vitoria International; vitoriainternational.com. **Container with wooden spoons, vase, and salt and butter dishes:** Williams Sonoma; williams-sonoma.com. **Island sink faucet** "Victorian Pull-Out Kitchen Faucet" in polished chrome: DXV; dxv.com. **Island sink** Portsmouth collection in stainless steel: American Standard; americanstandard-us.com. **Bar stools** "Crin" by Steven Volpe: McGuire Furniture; mcguirefurniture.com. **Wall clock:** vintage: French Metro Antiques; frenchmetro.com. **Curtains** custom, "Yuti" fabric by Anthology in Pewter and Charcoal: Style Library; stylelibrary.com. **Lamp** "Castle Peak" by Kate Spade: Circa Lighting; circalighting. com. **Carpet:** Feizy Rugs; feizy.com. **Artwork over sink** "Agua Viva" series: Aldara Ortega; aloarts.com. **Light over artwork** "Dorchester 24-inch Picture Light" by E.F. Chapman: Circa Lighting; circalighting.com. **Perimeter sink faucet** "Fresno Culinary Kitchen Faucet" in polished chrome: DXV; dxv.com. **Perimeter sink** Portsmouth collection undermount in

stainless steel: American Standard; americanstandard-us.com.
BUTLER'S PANTRY — **Wall and cabinet paint** "Tavern Gray": Benjamin Moore; benjaminmoore.com. **Light fixture** "Yves Crystal Single-Arm Sconce" by Thomas O'Brien: Circa Lighting; circalighting.com. **Cabinets** Tupper Builders Inc.; 843/864-3615. **Drawer pulls** "Westwood" in satin brass: Emtek; emtek.com. **Glass shelving:** Glass Act Productions; glassactproductions.com. **Countertop** marble: Vitoria International; vitoriainternational.com. **Faucet** "Victorian Bar Faucet" in polished chrome: DXV; dxv.com. **Wine cooler** 24-inch undercounter wine reserve with glass door: Thermador; thermador.com.

PAGE 80. MASTER BEDROOM — **Interior designer:** Mary Douglas Drysdale, 2026 R St. NW, Washington, DC 20009; 202/588-0700; marydouglasdrysdale.com. **Ceiling paint** "Capitol White," **wall paint** "Ashwood Moss" 1484: Benjamin Moore; benjaminmoore.com. **Chandelier** "Cloud 37": Apparatus; apparatusstudio.com. **Bed** custom: Theodore Alexander; theodorealexander.com. **Gray stool:** Mary Douglas Drysdale; marydouglasdrysdale.com. **Carpet** "Tiago": Stark Carpet; starkcarpet.com. **Art over bed:** Hemphill Fine Arts; hemphillfinearts.com. **Black-patterned pillows** custom "BX 00044500" in Meteor by Old World Weavers: Scalamandre; scalamandre.com. **Black-and-ivory pillow in center:** Mary Douglas Drysdale; marydouglasdrysdale.com. **Sheets and comforter:** custom: Talini Home; talinihome.com. **Striped throw** "Aberdeen" in Dark Grey and Charcoal: Alicia Adams Alpaca; aliciaadamsalpaca.com. **Lamp** "Miller": Fritz Porter; fritzporter.com. **Black-and-white vase:** Sam Scott Pottery; samscottpottery.com. **Artwork at left** Codified 1 and Codified 5 by Julie Wolfe: Hemphill Fine Arts; hemphillfinearts.com. **Mirror** "Monroe": Theodore Alexander; theodorealexander.com. **Metal horses, black-and-white stool:** Mary Douglas Drysdale; marydouglasdrysdale.com. **Crumpled vase:** Doug Frates Glass; dougfratesglass.com.

PAGES 80–81. MASTER BATH SUITE — **Interior designer:** Ili Hidalgo-Nilsson, Terracotta Design Build Co., 403 W. Ponce de Leon Ave., Suite 215, Decatur, GA 30030; 404/377-0906; ili@terracottadesignbuild.com.
HALLWAY — **Ceiling paint** "Bruton White CW-710," **wall paint** "Randolph Gray" CW-85: Benjamin Moore; benjaminmoore.com. **Artwork** Brilljant by Brandon Luther: Southern Bit; southernbit.com. **Lights flanking artwork:** French vintage. **Rug** antique Oushak: Sharian Inc.; sharian.com. SHOWER — **Ceiling tile** "Snow Flower" from the Yin + Yang collection, **wall tile** "Laminam Porcelain" in Argento: Crossville; crossvilleinc.com. **Showerheads** "Modulus" 7½-inch in polished chrome: DXV; dxv.com. **Marble on walls and bench** "State of Grace" porcelain slab: Crossville; crossvilleinc.com. **Chair** "Royd Accent Chair" in gold, **black figures on bench** "Hagan," **octopus** "Paul" in shiny gold brass: Made Goods; madegoods.com. **Shower valves** "Equility"

DESIGN FILE

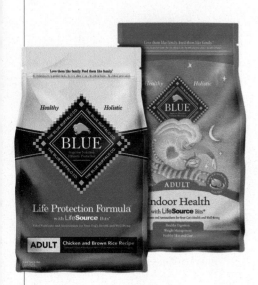

Healthy and Tasty Pet Food

Blue Buffalo® pet food always

starts with real meat and includes

garden veggies and fruit.

Compare your pet food to

BLUE at TrueBLUETest.com

wall valve trim and thermostatic valve trim in polished chrome, **hand shower** "Equility" shower set with hand shower in polished chrome: DXV; dxv.com. **Floor tile** "Black Dragon" and "Snow Flower" stack mosaic: Crossville; crossvilleinc.com. TUB NICHE—**Ceiling paint** "Bruton White" CW-710 in high gloss, **Wall, baseboard, and crown molding paint** "Randolph Gray" CW-85: Benjamin Moore; benjaminmoore.com. **Bathtub** "Equality Slim Freestanding Soaking Tub" in Canvas White, **faucet** "Square Water-Saving Floor-Mount Bathtub Faucet" in polished chrome: DXV; dxv.com. **Bathtub tray** "Maison Storage Bath Caddy" in Antique Brass: Anthropologie; anthropologie.com. **Chandelier** "Hampton Medium" by Aerin in Plaster White: Circa Lighting; circalighting.com. **Roman shades** custom in white linen and black tape: Schumacher; fschumacher.com. **Framed artwork in window:** owner's collection. **Teardrop stool by bathtub** "Eada" in Cool Gray, **dish on stool** "Porter Bowl" in white marble: Made Goods; madegoods.com. **Gold spoon:** Found Co. Decatur; foundcodecatur.com. BEVERAGE STATION—**Cabinetry** design by Terracotta Design Build; terracottadesignbuild.com. **Drawer and door pulls** "Oomph" knobs, "Robin" and "District" pulls in brass: Lisa Jarvis; lisa-jarvis.com. **Refrigerator/freezer** 24-inch inch undercounter double drawers, custom panel-ready, **coffee machine** 24-inch built-in coffee machine with Home Connect: Thermador; thermador.com. VANITY—**Ceiling paint** "Bruton White" CW-710, **wall paint** "Randolph Gray" CW-85: Benjamin Moore; benjaminmoore.com. **Wallpaper behind mirrors** "Envisioned M" in Platinum: Kravet; kravet.com. **Mirrors** "Ariela" in Vintage Gray: Made Goods; madegoods.com. **Lights flanking mirrors** "Alpine Sconce" in hand-rubbed Antique Brass: Circa Lighting; circalighting.com. **Vine corbel on wall:** antique. **Towel holder** "Percy" small towel bar in chrome: DXV; dxv.com. **Countertop** "Film Noir Unpolished" porcelain: Crossville; crossvilleinc.com. **Cabinetry:** design by Terracotta Design Build; terracottadesignbuild.com. **Drawer and door pulls** "Oomph" knobs and "Robin" pulls in brass: Lisa Jarvis; lisa-jarvis.com. **Sinks** "Webster" undercounter in white; **faucets** "Equality" widespread bathroom faucet: DXV; dxv.com. **Magnifying mirror:** antique. **Framed racehorse prints** *Basel & Murano:* Made Goods; madegoods.com. **PAGES 82–83.** LADIES' DRAWING ROOM—**Interior designer:** Mallory Mathison Glenn, 452 E. Paces Ferry Road NE, Atlanta, GA 30305; 404/816-3860; mallorymathison.com. **Ceiling paint** "Nelson Blue" CW-635 in eggshell finish, **wall, trim, and fireplace paint** "Claret" CW-305 in high-gloss: Benjamin Moore; benjaminmoore.com. **Chandelier** "Venetian 28-inch Candle Style" in hand-rubbed Antique Brass: Circa Lighting; circalighting.com. **Shades on chandelier** custom: Lamp Arts, Inc.; lampartsinc.com. **Painting over fireplace:** William McLure; williammclure.com. **Green vases, black bust, and fire screen:** designer's own. **Blue-and-white chairs** "756

Declan": Wesley Hall; wesleyhall.com. **Chair fabric** "Rajah Blue Velvet,"**chair trim** "Nura" in Glacier by Manuel Canovas, **bottom trim** "Pavilion Wide Braid" in Aqua: Cowtan & Tout; cowtan.com. **Ottoman** "Eden" 15C: Wesley Hall; wesleyhall.com. **Ottoman fabric** "Marbella" in Rose: Cowtan & Tout; cowtan.com. **Trim** "2.5-inch Normandy Silk Crete" in Printemps-23: Samuel and Sons; samuelandsons.com. **Pillows on chairs** custom "Nanda" in Jonquille by Manuel Canovas; Cowtan & Tout; cowtan.com. **Gold tables** "Hand-Forged Martini Table" by Studio VC: Circa Lighting; circalighting.com. **Painting over bookcase** *Neighborhood Culture* by Sara Lawson: Mallory Mathison; mallorymathison.com. **Drapery hardware:** custom. **Drapery fabrics** "Diane-Nattier" by Manuel Canovas; **banding** "Genoa" in pink by Colefax & Fowler: Cowtan & Tout; cowtan.com. **Shades under draperies:** custom. **Floor lamp** "Dorchester Swing-Arm Lamp" in brass: Circa Lighting; circalighting.com. **Shade** custom: Mallory Mathison; mallorymathison.com. **Desk** antique: Parc Monceau; parcmonceauatl.com. **Desk chair** "Rowan Side Chair" in Mont Blanc Bermuda leather with tape trim: Wesley Hall; wesleyhall.com. **Artwork over desk, items on desk, and statue in window:** designer's own. **White wicker chair:** vintage. **Chair fabric** "Timbuktu Velvet" by Lee Jofa: Kravet; kravet.com. **Needlepoint pillow** "I would prefer not to": Lycette Designs; lycettedesigns.com. **Cocktail table** custom: Gracie Studio; graciestudio.com. **Blue sofa** custom: Mallory Mathison; mallorymathison.com. **Sofa fabric** "Linen Velvet" in Aqua: Cowtan & Tout; cowtan.com. **Oriental pillows** custom, "B7553001 Cochinchine" in Gris Bleu: Pierre Frey; pierrefrey.com. **Lamp** "Suzanne" in Blush Pink: Christopher Spitzmiller; christopherspitzmiller.com. **Blue rug:** Moattar, Ltd.; moattar.com. **Woven rush mat under rug:** available in custom sizing: Mallory Mathison; mallorymathison.com.

PAGE 83. MEZZANINE—**Interior designer:** Charlotte Lucas, 416 Providence Road Suite 3, Charlotte, NC 28207; 980/859-7499; charlottelucasdesign.com. **Paint on shutters** "Polo Blue" 2062-10: Benjamin Moore; benjaminmoore.com. **Metal plant containers on lattice:** vintage. **Side table** "Parc End Table": Woodard Furniture; woodard-furniture.com. **Table paint** "Habanero Pepper" 1306: Benjamin Moore; benjaminmoore.com. **Woven tray:** no longer available. **Colored ceramic balls** *Spheres* by Virginia Scotchie: Hidell Brooks Gallery; hidellbrooks.com. **Chairs** "Cane Swivel Rocking Lounge Chair": Woodard Furniture; woodard-furniture.com. **Chair fabric** "Magical Menagerie" in Primary: Schumacher; fschumacher.com. **Pillow** custom, in Valdese/Fletcher/Cherry: Valdese Weavers; valdeseweavers.com. **Peacock:** vintage. **Floor base coat** Super Spek industrial enamel, **diamond paint** "Mopboard Black": Benjamin Moore; benjaminmoore.com.

TRADITIONAL HOME®
DESIGN FILE

OUR FAVORITE EVENTS, PRODUCTS + PROMOTIONS

DISCOVER ADAC
September 24-26, 2019

With a program spanning keynote presentations, salon-style talks, book signings, sip and strolls, and more, this celebration connects a national audience of design authorities, enthusiasts, and media. Unlock potential, break boundaries, explore new sources of inspiration, reveal unseen possibilities, and create a vision that is authentic to you. Registration Now Open
adacatlanta.com/discover-adac/

#DISCOVERADAC | @adacatlanta

ADAC

TIMELESSLEE 50

Since 1969 LEE Industries has been manufacturing handcrafted, American-made furniture. We are committed to bringing innovative upholstery and earth-friendly products to the design community through custom styles and awe-inspiring fabrics. We are delighted to celebrate nearly 50 years in creating timeless LEE classics through cutting-edge design and sustainable processes.

leeindustries.com

KingsHaven.
Get inspired.

KingsHaven designs handmade lighting, furnishings and decorative accessories for residential, hospitality and commercial settings. KingsHaven's products are created with exceptional craftsmanship by talented artisans. Hand-forged iron and wood-crafted lighting ranges from historic reproductions of fine European antiques to more modern traditional, transitional and contemporary designs. Many stylish, in-stock selections are available for expedited shipping. KingsHaven also provides bespoke finishes, virtually any color choice, and fully custom options to suit all interior or outdoor space design themes.

Pictured: Metrique Pendant.
Learn more: www.KingsHaven.com.

A Pop of Personality

From eye-catching patterned encaustics to statement art glass, our expansive new color collections offer endless options to make your space uniquely yours. You'll never get lost in a sea of white subway tile again.

Schedule a complimentary design consultation or visit a store today.

tileshop.com

The Tile Shop

LEE 50

KINGS⬥HAVEN

PAGES 84–85. CARRIAGE HOUSE GUEST SUITE— **Interior designer:** Olivia Brock, 343 E. Bay St., Charleston, SC 29401; 843/900-0430; Torrance Mitchell Designs; torrancemitchell.com. **Wall paint** "Elmire White" HC-84; **window trim paint** "Salisbury Green" HC-139: Benjamin Moore; benjaminmoore.com. **Curtain hardware, woven rug:** Torrance Mitchell Designs; torrancemitchell.com. **Abstract art between windows** by Way Way Allen: Charleston Artist Collective; charlestonartistcollective.org. **Café curtains** Kravet Basics 30817-1 in white, **trim** "Laine Print" by Lee Jofa in Pacific 2017169.13: Kravet; kravet.com. **Bed** "Camden Untufted Bed": Ballard Designs; ballarddesigns.com. **Bed upholstery fabric** "Laine Print" by Lee Jofa in Pacific 2017169.13: Kravet; kravet.com. **Bed linens** "Suzanne Kasler Positano Sheet Set" in Sky, **comforter** "Arabesque Embroidered Quilt" in Soft White, **footstool** "Miles Redd Paw Perching Stool": Ballard Designs; ballarddesigns.com. **Stool fabric** "Carsten Check" in Pale Blue and Cream" by Brunschwig & Fils: Kravet; kravet.com. **Decorative pillows** "Fabriano Cotton and Linen Print" in Grey by Brunschwig & Fils: Kravet; kravet.com. **Lamps on nightstands** "Dorchester Club": Circa Lighting; circalighting.com. **Art over headboard, breakfast tray, nightstand chests, hat, artwork of birds:** vintage. **Silver vase:** designer's own. **Chair by window** "Bunny Williams Regency Dining Chair," **throw** "Classic Herringbone" in Olive: Ballard Designs; ballarddesigns.com.

PAGE 85. BATHROOM— **Interior designers:** Michael Mitchell and Tyler Hill, 438 King St., Charleston, SC 29403; 843/564-0034; mitchellhillinc.com. **Stylist:** Olivia Brock; torrancemitchell.com. **Lighting** "Hulton Sconce" by Thomas O'Brien: Circa Lighting; circalighting.com. **Shower lever** "Randall Pressure Balanced Shower Valve Trim with Lever Handle" in satin brass, **toilet** "St. George Two-Piece Elongated Toilet" in Canvas White, **sink** "Oakhill Console Sink" in Canvas White/satin brass, **faucet** "Oak Hill Wall-Mount with Cross Handles" in satin brass: DXV; dxv.com. **Tile** "Snow Flower" and "Black Dragon" from the Yin + Yang collection linear and stacked mosaics, **shower floor** 1/2×1/2-inch mosaic white: Crossville; crossvilleinc.com. **Shower door and hardware:** Emtek; emtek.com. **Mirror** "Halstad" in antique gold: Ballard Designs; ballarddesigns.com.

PAGE 86. LEOPARD'S DEN— **Interior designer:** Angie Hranowsky, 128 Wentworth St., No. 2, Charleston, SC 29401; 843/810-3286; angiehranowsky.com. **Upholstered wall, ceiling, lampshade fabric** "Sabu 0314-04" in Red Rose by Rose Cumming: Ainsworth Noah + Associates; ainsworth-noah.com. **Cornice, drapery, headboard, and bed-skirt fabric** "Dot SPL-4100-30" in Fern: Sister Parish Design; sisterparishdesign.com. **Cornice and drapery trim** "Palolem SE01054 Au Bout de la Nuit": Elitis, Inc.; elitis.fr. **Window frame and bookcase paint** "Black Raspberry" 2072-20: Benjamin Moore; benjaminmoore.com. **Lamps with pink shades** "Alex" in Aubergine: Christopher Spitzmiller; christopherspitzmiller.com. **Lampshades** custom in "Anjuna Vintage Pink": Elitis, Inc.; elitis.fr. **Table under right lamp:** antique. **Floor lamp** "Hackney" in hand-rubbed Antique Brass: Circa Lighting; circalighting.com. **Chair** antique: Elizabeth Stuart Design; elizabethstuartdesign.com. **Bed:** vintage. **Green pillows** custom, "Avant GWF3531.308" in green and black by Lee Jofa: Kravet; kravet.com. **Pink pillow** custom, "Aurel" in Rose: Decors Barbares; decorsbarbares.com. **Throw** "abcDNA Om Throw" in orange rust: ABC Carpet + Home; abchome.com. **Comforter, bed linens** Triomphe collection in Blanc; Yves Delorme; yvesdelorme.com. **Bench:** vintage. **Bench fabric** "Madras Floral Willow" in Linen: Maresca Textiles; marescatextiles.com. **Black-and-white chair:** vintage. **Chair fabric** "Dinisen" in Smoke by Lee Jofa: Kravet; kravet.com. **Pillow on chair** custom, "AK0744 Bosforo 012" in purple velvet: Brochier; brochier.it. **Fringe on pillow** "Pin017 Rouche Col.5" in Violetta-Aragosta: Dedar; dedar.com. **Woven rug** "Aparri–Wild Rice": Merida Studio; meridastudio.com. DOOR DETAIL—**Paint** "Black Raspberry": Benjamin Moore; benjaminmoore.com. **Door knobs** "Norwich" in French Antique finish: Emtek; emtek.com.

PAGE 87. ARTIST'S STUDIO & BATH—**Interior designer:** Cameron Schwabenton, Cameron Stewart Interior Design, 164 Market St., #375, Charleston, SC 29401; 843/ 352-2532; info@cameronstewartdesign.com. **Wall and ceiling paint** "Orleans Violet," **window sash paint** "Midnight Oil": Benjamin Moore; benjaminmoore.com. **Chair** vintage midcentury chair upholstered in "Providence" T1017/02 cream: Weitzner; weitznerlimited.com. **Pink pillow:** custom-made from vintage saris. **Ottoman** custom: Cameron Schwabenton; info@cameronstewartdesign.com. **Ottoman trim** "Greek Key Braid" in Wisteria: Robert Allen Design; robertallendesign.com. **Tray on ottoman, mailbox, and wall cameos:** vintage. **Draperies** custom, "Obsession" velvet fabric in Aegean: P Kaufmann Fabrics; available at fabric.com. **Tiebacks** custom-made from Civil War-era epaulets: Cameron Schwabenton; info@cameronstewart design.com. BATH—**Wall paint** "Orleans Violet": Benjamin Moore; benjamin moore.com. **Wall sconce** "Marlborough Single Sconce" in gilded iron: Circa Lighting; circalighting.com. **Metal vase with duck feather fans:** vintage. **Faucet** "Ashbee Widespread Bathroom Faucet with Lever Handles" in polished chrome, **sink** "Pop Grande Oval Undercounter" in Canvas White: DXV; dxv.com. **Countertop** "Black Tie Polished" porcelain: Crossville; crossvilleinc.com. **Fabric for sink skirt** "Mandarin Sheer" in Ironwork: Pollack Fabric; pollackassociates.com.

PAGES 88–95
KITCHEN 2.0
Architect: Michael Abraham, Clarendon Hills, Illinois; 630/655-9417; contacts@michael-abraham.com; michael-abraham.com.

Designer: Mick De Giulio, De Giulio Kitchen Design, Chicago; 312/494-9200; degiuliodesign.com. **Interior design:** Yoanna Kulas; 847-853-5200. **THROUGHOUT. Flooring** white oak: contact local flooring suppliers. **Wall paint** "Decorator's White": Benjamin Moore; benjaminmoore.com.
PAGES 88–89, 92–93. KITCHEN—**Cabinetry** rift-cut white oak plank in white opaque finish, **white hardware, cooking table** white oak, **oven console** in brushed stainless steel, **sink** honed white Carrara marble and brushed stainless steel with sliding teak cutting board, **freestanding étagère and hanging plate rack** in hot-rolled steel, **hood**: De Giulio Collection; degiuliodesign.com/collections. **Countertops** honed white Carrara marble: contact local cut-stone suppliers. **Island sink faucet** "Tara Ultra" in chrome, **perimeter sink faucet** "Single-Lever Mixer": Dornbracht; dornbracht.com. **Refrigerators, cooktop, single oven, convection oven, warming drawer:** Sub-Zero; subzero-wolf.com. **Dishwashers** integrated with island, **perimeter cabinets:** Miele; mieleusa.com. **Dining table and bench** "Paradou," **bar stools** "Alexander": AM Designs; amdesigns.com. **Sconces:** Delta Light; deltalight.us. BUTLER'S PANTRY—**Sink faucet** "Vir Stil" by Laura Kirar: Kallista; kallista.com.
PAGES 90–91. LIVING ROOM—**Chairs, wooden tables, large ottoman** all custom: Malibu Market & Design; malibumarketdesign.com. **White-lacquered wood logs:** Gervasoni; gervasoni1882.it. **Rug** vintage Turkish hemp: homeowners' collection. **Artwork in hallway:** Wesley Kimler Studio; wesleykimlerstudio.com.
PAGES 94–95. CLOSET—**Ottoman:** Rachel Ashwell; shabbychic.com. BEDROOM—**Bed** custom: Rachel Ashwell; shabbychic.com. **Chair** "Ghost 01," **ottoman** "Ghost 06P": Gervasoni; gervasoni1882.it. **Side table:** Malibu Market & Design; malibumarketdesign.com. **Exterior fence:** Post & Picket; postandpicket.com. SHOWER—**Floor and walls** honed white Carrara marble: contact local cut-stone

suppliers. **Faucet** "Tara Logic" in Matte Platinum: Dornbracht; dornbracht.com. **Shower doors:** Bianco Glass Products; biancoglass.com. BATH—**Tub** "Ovale" in Matte White: Lacava; lacava.com. **Faucet** "Tara Logic" in Matte Platinum: Dornbracht; dornbracht.com. **Shower enclosure, mirror:** Bianco Glass Products; biancoglass.com. **Sink** "Original" by Barbara Barry in Stucco White: Kallista; kallista.com. **Side table:** Malibu Market & Design; malibumarketdesign.com. **Floor-mounted towel warmer:** Artos; artos-store.com.

PAGES 96–107
LIGHT AT HEART
Interior designer: Ray Booth, McAlpine, Nashville; 615/259-1222; mcalpinehouse.com.
PAGES 97–99. ENTRYWAY—**Drapery fabric** "Nottingham White": Holland & Sherry; interiors.hollandandsherry.com. **Chandelier** "Chambord": Dennis & Leen; dennisandleen.com. **Ottoman fabric:** Claremont; claremontfurnishing.com. **White chair** "Rosalind": Madeline Stuart; madelinestuart.com. **Fabric for chair pillow** "Dune Mirage": Brentano; brentanofabrics.com. **Throw:** R. Hughes; r-hughes.com. **Upholstered chair with wooden arms** "Queen Anne Walnut Armchair": Carl Moore Antiques; carlmooreantiques.com. **Chair fabric** "Porcini Chenille" in Laguna: Sabina Fay Braxton; sabinafaybraxton.com. **Rug** "Arman": Tai Ping; taipingtent.com. **Bowl on center table** "Sculptural Lucite Centerpiece bowl": Assemblage; assemblageltd.1stdibs.com. **Sofa** "Princeton": Ferrell Mittman; ferrellmittman.com. **Sofa fabric** "Sandcastle" in Fleur de Sel: Holly Hunt; hollyhunt.com. **Ottomans** "Mia": Stewart Furniture; stewartfurniture.com. **Sofa pillow fabric** "Kohtan Perle": Castel; castelmaison.com. **Flange tape** 32421-9020: Houlès; houles.com. **Table at French doors** custom: through McAlpine; mcalpinehouse.com. **Table lamp** "Silverplate Column": Sentimento; sentimentoantiques.1stdibs.com. **Chair at table** "Supper Room": Soane; soane.co.uk. **Chair leather** "Stingray" in Ivory Coast: Holly Hunt; hollyhunt.com. **Artwork on table** *Ice Age No. 643* ink, silk and beeswax on panel: Eric Blum; ericblum.net. CONSERVATORY—**Drapery fabric** "Mayo" in Ecru: Loro Piana; us.loropiana.com. **Slipcovered sofa** "Paige" by Kerry Joyce: Dessin Fournir; dessinfournir.com. **Slipcover fabric** "Alcott Willow": Pindler; pindler.com. **Floor lamp** "Tolomeo Mega": Artimede; artimede.com. **Table lamp** polished steel: Sentimento; sentimentoantiques.1stdibs.com. **Large table** "Oak Gateleg": Lucca & Co.; luccany.com. **Tan chair** "Grand Lounger Skirted Chair" by McAlpine Home: Lee Industries; leeindustries.com. **Striped pillow fabric** "Burlington" by Hodsoll McKenzie: Zimmer + Rohde; zimmer-rohde.com. **Pair of chairs** "Tucker": Gemelli; gemellireproductions.com. **Chair fabric** "Linara Manilla": Romo; romo.com. **Table with vase of blue flowers** "English Cricket Table": Gregorius Pineo; gregoriuspineo.com. **Round side table** "Cavallo": David

Iatesta; davidiatesta.com. **Rug** "Rumi Fretwork": Tai Ping; taipingtent.com.
PAGES 100–101. LIVING ROOM—**Sofa:** Lucca & Co.; luccany.com. **Ottoman** "Cockerel": George Smith; georgesmith.com. **Patterned chair** "Cushion Chair": Soane: soane.co.uk. **Chair fabric** Bergamo: Donghia; donghia.com. **Matching chairs** "Bowen": Dessin Fournir; dessinfournir.com. **Chair fabric** "Sydney," **love-seat fabric** "Hardwick" by Hodsoll McKenzie: Zimmer + Rohde; zimmer-rohde.com. **Love seat** "Clermont," **lavender bench** "Trebizond": Ferrell Mittman; ferrellmittman.com. **Bench fabric** "Salina Marrone" by Fadini Borghi: Pierre Frey; pierrefrey.com. **Footstool:** Sentimento; sentimentoantiques .1stdibs.com. **Floor lamp:** Dixon Lane Antiques; 914/366-6090. **Console table at window** custom: McAlpine; mcalpinehouse.com. **Artwork above sofa** *Central Park I* by Tom Brydelsky: Tinney Contemporary; tinneycontemporary.com. **Drapery fabric** "Fredericka": Nancy Corzine; nancycorzine.com. DINING ROOM—**Long table** custom: McAlpine; mcalpinehouse.com. **Table fabrication:** Mitchell Yanosky; mitchellyanosky.com. **Chairs** "Supper Room" in Walnut Coco de Mer, **sconce:** Soane; soane.co.uk. **Chair leather** "Stingray" in Ivory Coast: Holly Hunt; hollyhunt.com. **Artwork above slipcovered chair** *Oil on Aluminum Panel*: Tyrell Collins; tyrellcollins.com. **Artwork at windows** *Untitled:* David Kidd; davidkiddpaintings.com. **Table at draperies** ironwood with shaped skirt, **mirror** Cassetta Form: Sentimento; sentimentoantiques.1stdibs.com. **Neoclassical floor lamp:** Cote Jardin Antiques; cotejardinantiques.com. **Slipcovered chair** "Albert": Dessin Fournir; dessinfournir.com. **Slipcover fabric** "Linara" in Antique White: Romo; romo.com. **Drapery fabric** "Brandy and Cashew" by B. Berger: Duralee; duralee.com. **Cabinet and fireplace:** McAlpine; mcalpinehouse.com. **Library lights:** Besselink & Jones; besselink.com. **Round table** "Trittico": Gregorius Pineo; gregoriuspineo.com. **Dark velvet chair** "Sylvan": Ferrell Mittman; ferrellmittman.com. **Settee** "Gabrielle":

READER'S RESOURCE

Niermann Weeks; niermannweeks.com. **Candlesticks:** Aero; aerostudios.com. **Chandelier** "Russian": Dennis & Leen; dennisandleen.com. **PAGES 102–103.** KITCHEN—**Range:** Lacanche; lacanche.fr. **Flooring** Torros black and Kemelpasa white marble in tumbled finish, **countertops and backsplash** statuary marble: contact local cut-stone suppliers. **Range hood** custom: McAlpine; mcalpinehouse.com. **Refrigerators:** Sub-Zero; subzero-wolf.com. **Counter stools:** MacRae; macraedesigns.com. **Settee** custom: Lee Industries; leeindustries.com. **Chair** "Albert": Dessin Fournir; dessinfournir.com. **Oval cherry drop-leaf table:** Beaman Antiques; beamanantiques.com. **Pendant** "Graydon" in polished nickel: Lona Design; lonadesign.com. **Copper pots:** Sentimento; entimentoantiques.1stdibs.com. **PAGES 104–105.** MASTER BEDROOM—**Chandelier** "Arctic Pear," **chaise longue** "Divine Recline": Ochre; ochre.net. **Bed** "Arca": Switch Modern; switchmodern.com. **Benches** "Waisted" custom, **bedside tables** custom: McAlpine; mcalpinehouse.com. **Small round table at daybed** "Cygnet": David Iatesta; davidiatesta.com. **Daybed pillow fabric** "Winhurst": Pindler; pindler. com. **Duvet and shams** "Osaka Wisteria," **white bedcover** "Savoy Ivory Coverlet": Nancy Koltes; nancykoltes.com. **Floor lamp:** Lucca & Co.; luccany.com. **Rug** custom Revanche collection "Hybride": Tai Ping; taipingtent.com. MASTER BATH—**Tub** "Candide": Waterworks; waterworks.com. **Floor tile** custom pattern in statuary and logos azul marble: contact local cut-stone suppliers. **Chair:** Mattaliano; mattaliano.com. **Floor lamp** "Tripod": Hinson Lighting; hinsonlighting.com. **Chandelier** "Jaeger" custom: Ironies; ironies.com. EXTERIOR—**Driveway** salt-and-pepper cobblestone: contact local cut-stone suppliers. **PAGES 106–107.** PORCH AND LAWN—**White chairs** "Plantation": Uwharrie; uwharriechair. com. **Flooring** bluestone: contact local cut-stone suppliers. **Sofa and chairs** "Gibbings" in teak: Michael Taylor Designs; michaeltaylordesigns.com. **Drapery fabric** "Mist" in Snow: Silver State; silverstatetextiles.com. **Coffee tables** tiered marble-and-iron tables, **garden stool, mirror:** homeowners' collection. **Swing** custom: McAlpine; mcalpinehouse.com.

PAGES 108–117
BEST OF BOTH

Interior designer: Amy Meier; Amy Meier Design, Rancho Santa Fe, California; 858/848-4151; amymeier.com. **Architectural designer:** Bartanyi A. Endre, Del Mar, California; 858/755-6005. **Builder:** Tony Parker, Tony Parker General Builders, Poway, California; 858/391-1430. **PAGES 108–109.** LIVING ROOM—**Wall paint** "Paper White": Benjamin Moore; benjaminmoore.com. **Chairs at coffee table** "Rising Moon": Rose Tarlow; rosetarlow.com. **Chair fabric** Jasper collection: Michael S Smith Inc.; michaelsmithinc.com. **Coffee table** custom, **chair at mantel** antique: Amy Meier Design; amymeier.com. **Material for coffee table**

"Silestone": Cosentino; silestoneusa.com. **Fireplace mantel:** Chateau Domingue; chateaudomingue.com. **Sconce** vintage "Serge Roche": homeowners' collection. **Andirons:** Ironware International; ironware international.com. **Pendant:** Liz's Antique Hardware; lahardware.com. **Rug:** Loro Piana; us.loropiana.com. **PAGES 110–111.** DINING ROOM—**Table** custom, **chairs** vintage Italian: homeowners' collection. **Chair fabric:** Kravet; kravet.com. **Cabinet hardware:** Chicago Brass; chicagobrass.com. **Pendant** "Dover Ball": Urban Electric; urbanelectric.com. **Items in glass cabinet:** David Alan Collection; hedavidalancollection.com. ENTRY—**Sconces:** Visual Comfort through Circa Lighting; circalighting.com. **Stair runner:** Stark Carpet; starkcarpet.com. **Antique sugar bins:** homeowners' collection. EXTERIOR—**Lanterns:** Bevolo Gas & Electric Lights; bevolo.com. **PAGES 112–113.** KITCHEN—**Pendants** "Helio," **sink faucets:** Waterworks; waterworks.com. **Dining chairs** vintage: Leif; leifalmont.com. **Bar stools** custom, **dining table** antique French wine tasting table: homeowners' collection. **PAGES 114–115.** MASTER BEDROOM—**Bed:** Boiler & Co.; boilerco.com. **Bedding:** Matouk; matouk.com. **Lamp:** William Lamen; williamlamen.com. **Bench** French antique: homeowners' collection. **Bench fabric** "Medici" by Classic Cloth: Dessin Fournir; dessinfournir.com. **Artwork** by James Austin Murray: Madison Gallery; madisongalleries.com. **Plaster mirror:** Amy Meier Design; amymeier.com. **Rug:** Stark Carpet; starkcarpet.com. **Window treatment fabric:** Kravet; kravet.com. **PAGES 116–117.** MASTER BATH—**Vanity** "Drapier Table": Cest la Vie Antiques; cestlavieantiques.com. **Tub** "Candide," **faucets:** Waterworks; waterworks.com. **Sinks:** Kohler; us.kohler.com. **Sconces:** Avrett; avrett.com.

Winter 2019 issue
on sale October 25

THE SOURCE

Like what you saw in Traditional Home this month? Here's your chance to learn more!

Request product information and learn more about the featured brands and products using one of the following methods:

- Return the coupon on this page
- Visit traditionalhome.com/source

You'll receive exclusive advertiser information and be on your way to designing the home of your dreams.

CR LAINE FURNITURE
World-friendly custom upholstery handcrafted by artisans in North Carolina utilizing new processes and equipment while holding true to time-tested premium construction features since 1958. Our distinct blend of style, comfort, and color delivers a classic aesthetic with a modern perspective. For ideas and inspiration visit us online at www.crlaine.com.

5

CROSSVILLE
Crossville Porcelain Countertops are here! Enjoy all the advantages of porcelain tile for your countertops: stunning styles in polished or unpolished finishes, incredible durability, and no stains, cracks, or yellowing. These versatile 12mm slabs come in a bevy of sophisticated looks to meet your design vision. Explore the options of this countertop alternative at crossvilleinc.com.

6

DACOR
24" Integrated Full-Size Wine Cellar. Easily holds up to 100 bottles of wine in three independently cooled zones, perfectly stored behind a triple layer of argon gas filled glass to protect your collection from harmful UV and IR light. Panel-ready for graphite, stainless steel or custom panels and with option for handle-free push-to-open door.

7

FERGUSON BATH, KITCHEN & LIGHTING GALLERY
Allow Ferguson to be the solution for your plumbing, lighting and appliance needs. We offer the best selection of products, like the Robertson Vanity in white by Signature Hardware. Visit fergusonshowrooms.com to find the showroom nearest you.

8

GABBY
When it comes to transitional furniture and lighting in eclectic, vintage, modern and antique style, Gabby pushes the envelope to find the most beautiful materials and designs. Gabby creates compelling products, including accent furniture, dining and occasional tables, chairs, mirrors, and US-made custom upholstery to furnish graceful homes for everyday living.
www.gabbyhome.com

9

KINGS•HAVEN
KingsHaven designs handmade lighting, decorative accessories and furniture with current relevance, exceptional details and uncompromising craftsmanship. Made of hand-forged iron, exotic woods, and finely selected materials, products range from historic reproductions to transitional and modern styling. KingsHaven also offers fully customizable options.
www.KingsHaven.com

10

LEE INDUSTRIES
Inspired by the classics but committed to the future, LEE effortlessly blends quality and comfort with form and function to create upholstery that is so strikingly fresh you almost forget that it is sustainable. Handcrafted with pride in the USA! Free Mini-catalog. To view our entire collection, visit us at www.leeindustries.com.

11

LEXINGTON HOME BRANDS
We create fresh and innovative home furnishings in styles that will inspire—ranging from traditional to contemporary for spaces indoors and out. Explore our collections including Tommy Bahama Home, Barclay Butera, Artistica Home, and Sligh at lexington.com

12

MITCHELL GOLD + BOB WILLIAMS
Explore a refined collective of beloved favorites and sleek new silhouettes, reflective of our signature style and 30 years of design and innovation. Soothing neutrals and warm textures meld with beautifully patinaed leathers and polished metals, for a look that's timeless, yet timely. Join MG+BW Comfort Club for everyday savings and exclusive benefits for members and the trade. Details at mgbwhome.com.

13

REPLACEMENTS, LTD
At Replacements, we refresh and revive real-deal vintage tableware so you can set the scene for life's most meaningful moments. See how our lively patterns from the past can elevate every look and space. Explore what's possible at replacements.com.

14

THE SOURCE

If your items are free, detach and mail this coupon. **If there are charges for your items**, mail coupon and check or money order in U.S. dollars only to: Inquiry Management Systems, Inc., P.O.Box 5132, Buffalo, NY 14205-5132

Order By Mail:
- Circle your choices • Complete Information below
- Expired coupons will not be processed • Expiration date: 02/16/20
- Key Code: Dept TH1019IL

TO SUBSCRIBE TO TRADITIONAL HOME:
Circle No. S071 (1 Year U.S. $24.00.) Outside U.S. Circle No. S072 (1 year $34.00.)

1	Free	8	Free	15	Free
2	Free	9	Free	16	Free
3	Free	10	Free	17	Free
4	Free	11	Free		
5	Free	12	Free	S071	
6	Free	13	Free	S072	
7	Free	14	Free		

I AM ENCLOSING: $_____ TOTAL ENCLOSED

Are you planning to complete the following and if so, in which time frame? (circle all that apply)

Build:	0-3	3-6	6+ months
Remodel:	0-3	3-6	6+ months
Decorate:	0-3	3-6	6+ months
Add a room:	0-3	3-6	6+ months
Move:	0-3	3-6	6+ months

NAME

ADDRESS

CITY   STATE   ZIP

PHONE NO.

(OPTIONAL) E-MAIL ADDRESS
We will share your e-mail address with the advertisers from which you request information

THEODORE ALEXANDER
Theodore Alexander handcrafts furniture and accessories for your home with uncompromising quality, using the most interesting materials for both function and beauty. Our craftsmen seek to create products that will last for generations and will be a favorite in your home.
TheodoreAlexander.com

15

WESLEY HALL
For over 30 years, Wesley Hall has manufactured the industry's finest traditional and transitional upholstery silhouettes, offering consumers an amazing array of impeccably styled and beautifully finished options. Choose from over 1,500 fabrics, leathers and trims—or fall in love with the Chandler Chair pictured.
Classic Made Current.

16

WOODARD
The Art of the Patio. Woodard's timeless and classic furniture is built to outcomfort and overlast. From cozy club chairs to sprawling sun-soaked lounges and dining sets for two-to-ten, Woodard's quality and attention to detail will make your patio a masterpiece for years to come.
woodard-furniture.com

17

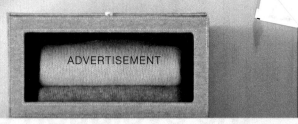
Elisabeth Moss
Actress known for her roles in *Mad Men*, *The Handmaid's Tale*, and her new movie, *The Kitchen*

Hometown I grew up in L.A. and now live in New York.

On the home front My home is a mix of antique and modern pieces, including a beautiful glass-and-brass coffee table I got at ABC Carpet & Home. I love Art Deco. And my only collection to speak of is a few paintings from an artist I love out of Brooklyn named Dan-ah Kim.

Kondo lite I love Marie Kondo, and although my version of it is somewhat bastardized and she would probably have a heart attack, it has helped me to be a little more organized! But sometimes there's still just a pile of clothes on the floor. Sorry, Marie.

Inside her closet It's actually pretty good right now, shockingly. I have it divided into dresses, skirts, and tops.

Chef's special Spaghetti, which is basically just boiling water.

Go-to party trick Staying home.

Best advice ever The power of the word "no" and how you shouldn't be afraid to use it.

I am traditional She has a huge soft spot for cats and spaghetti pomodoro, opts for a leather jacket and Chelsea boots when the weather's cool, is dying to learn to play the piano, and treasures a beautiful *Roman Holiday* poster from her mom and brother more than any other gift she's received.

TRADITIONAL HOME® (ISSN 883-4660), September/October 2019, Volume XXX Issue V, is published bimonthly in January/February, March/April, May/June, July/August, September/October, November/December 2019, by Meredith Corporation, 1716 Locust Street, Des Moines, IA 50309-3023. Periodicals postage paid at Des Moines, IA, and at additional mailing offices. Subscription prices, $24 per year in the U.S.; $32 (U.S. dollars) in Canada; $32 (U.S. dollars) overseas. POSTMASTER: Send all UAA to CFS. (See DMM 507.1.5.2); NON-POSTAL AND MILITARY FACILITIES: Send address corrections to Traditional Home Magazine, P.O. Box 37508, Boone, IA 50037-0508. In Canada: mailed under Publications Mail Sales Product Agreement No. 40069223; Canadian BN 12348 2867 RT. Your bank may provide updates to the card information we have on file. You may opt out of this service at any time. ©Meredith Corporation 2019. All rights reserved. Printed in the U.S.A.